Getting through to
your handicapped child

Getting through to
your handicapped child

A handbook for parents,
foster-parents, teachers and anyone
caring for handicapped children

ELIZABETH NEWSON

Joint Director, Child Development Research Unit,
University of Nottingham

TONY HIPGRAVE

Lecturer in Psychology, School of Social Work,
University of Leicester

CAMBRIDGE UNIVERSITY PRESS
Cambridge
London   New York   New Rochelle
Melbourne   Sydney

Published by the Press Syndicate of the University of Cambridge
The Pitt Building, Trumpington Street, Cambridge CB2 1RP
32 East 57th Street, New York, NY 10022, USA
296 Beaconsfield Parade, Middle Park, Melbourne 3206, Australia

© Cambridge University Press 1982

First published 1982

Printed in Great Britain
at the University Press, Cambridge

Library of Congress catalogue card number: 82-4310

British Library cataloguing in publication data

Newson, Elizabeth
Getting through to your handicapped child.
1. Handicapped children   2. Interpersonal
communication
I. Title   II. Hipgrave, Tony
362.4'088054   HV888

ISBN 0 521 27056 1

Contents

v

Contents

Contents

vii

About the authors

Elizabeth Newson is Joint Director, with her husband, of the Child Development Research Unit at Nottingham University. They have written many books and papers on child rearing in its social context; their book *Toys and playthings in development and remediation* (Penguin/Allen and Unwin/ Pantheon) sets the play needs of handicapped children into a perspective of how play contributes to any child's development.

Tony Hipgrave, a lecturer in psychology in the School of Social Work, Leicester University, trained as a developmental psychologist at Nottingham and was formerly a research officer there, working with Elizabeth Newson on flexible fostering schemes ('shared care') for handicapped children. He has published papers on fathers caring for their children alone, and is writing a book on specialist fostering. He has worked with deprived children, and, with Elizabeth Newson, has organised 'independence holidays' for handicapped children.

Acknowledgements

Our first thanks must go to Beryl West, Joy Rayner and Veronica Lowe, whose calm secretarial skills transformed successive untidy drafts in two handwritings into a handsome typescript.

We are grateful to Posy Simmonds for allowing us to use the story of Willy and his mother on page 17; to Sam Grainger whose skill produced the photographs; to Rod Ballard and to the Open University for quotations in Chapter 10; to Rod Ballard, Peter Barbor, Ann Brechin, Rosemary Evans, Denny Fransman and Hugh Jolly for their helpful comments on this chapter; to Phil Christie for allowing us to use a shortened form of his developmental checklist; and to Glenys Jones, Derek Wilson and Phil Christie who tried out the material for us at different stages. The nursing staff at Stretton Hall Hospital and the care staff at Sutherland House School were at various times guinea-pigs for the workshop course: our thanks to them. Special thanks are due to Natalie and her parents, no strangers to the workshop course, who allowed us to photograph them for the front cover.

We have benefited from the experience of numerous colleagues, including students past and present; and undoubtedly some of their ideas have been incorporated into our thinking and may appear here without acknowledgement. If so, we thank them and ask them to forgive us.

Finally, however, we have learned most of all from the many parents who over the years have worked with us in partnership for their children. Their resilience, inventiveness and common sense have been the motive force for this book. They and their children have taught us the major part of what we know. This handbook is gratefully dedicated to them: it is indeed their book as much as ours.

ix

What this book is about

This book is intended for anyone who feels that its title makes sense for their own situation: that is, anyone who is having difficulty in 'getting through' to the handicapped child they are involved with, and would like to do better. That means that it will be particularly of interest to people concerned with bringing up a mentally handicapped child; but it is likely to be helpful in some ways to parents of deaf or blind children, or of children with serious communication problems such as autism and dysphasia.

Most people who have lived with handicap know that handicapped children can be very rewarding – more so than may be obvious to outsiders. Equally, they can at times create greater problems and stress for their families than can easily be imagined. Those who care day by day for a handicapped child do not want pity: what they need are practical guidelines to help both adult and child, not merely to endure their life together, but to enjoy it and seize on its opportunities for growth.

As the title suggests, the overall theme of this book is *communication*: the development of understandings between handicapped children and those who live for most or part of the time with them. This is rather different from those approaches which emphasise training and control of children's behaviour. It is our strong belief that we need to build up, and maintain, all positive aspects of a relationship between a handicapped child and his care-givers. Understanding each other clearly is an important part of any success-ful relationship. To children who may already have considerable difficulty in making sense of the world around them, it is essential that the people closest to them should not add to the confusion more than they have to.

The vital feature of the behavioural approach outlined here, then, is its usefulness in making our messages to the child simple, direct and capable of being received by him; but we have tried to set this firmly in a framework of *person-to-person* communication, in which learning to get on *with each other* is what we are aiming for. So we have not put much emphasis on 'modifying the child's behaviour until it is acceptable to us'; we *have* emphasised finding

1   PN

ways to negotiate with the child in a form he can understand, and helping him to discover his own achievement and self-respect. Through all of this, we are hoping that parents, foster-parents and non-parents will be working as a team for the child, each with respect for the special contributions that the others can make. We are in fact looking for a language of partnership between those who care for a handicapped child as one of their own family, and those who have trained for the job.

Because we are trying to convey an approach – that is, a way of tackling a problem which can be used *creatively* by the reader in many different situations – we have tried to avoid the trap of suggesting too many specific solutions to specific difficulties. The 'recipe' method is not always the most helpful. To cover every problem with a recipe for action would need an encyclopaedia. Instead, we hope the reader will, by the end, understand the kind of thinking that needs to go into finding a practical solution, and will be able to deal sensibly, effectively and confidently with situations which don't appear in the book.

We ourselves have already tried out the material in this handbook in a number of ways. We originally intended it to be used by groups of parents and foster-parents, meeting regularly together as a 'workshop' with a professional 'leader' in order to work out ways of helping their own children. We know that there are many professionals who would be prepared to lead such a group, if only they had some kind of framework to start from, and we hope that many new groups will come into being as a result of making our own material available. We have also experimented with similar workshops led by professionals for colleagues who have day-by-day care of handicapped children – whether care staff, nurses or others. Finally, parents who do not have parent groups running in their areas may still find that the ideas discussed here can be put into practice even without the support of a group, and will at least help them to understand their child's problems more fully; again, the book has already been successfully tested in this way. We hope that some of these parents will be encouraged to find a local professional and organise workshops for themselves. Some notes on running a workshop are given in Appendix 4.

The handbook is divided into ten chapters, each of which, except the last, is in two parts: an introduction to ideas and ways of working, followed by a section (tinted for easy reference) entitled 'So what now?'. This, as the title suggests, carries further the ideas in the first section: both by giving examples of these ideas in action with children we have known, and by trying out practical exercises.

Throughout, we have tried to keep our language straightforward and simple, avoiding jargon so far as we possibly can. Readers will also find that we have chosen to refer to the child as 'he'. This is because we feel it would be tedious to use 'he or she' regularly; and since handicapped children are,

2

statistically, more likely to be male, 'he' seemed the more sensible one to choose in speaking of children of either sex. In the same way, we have used 'mother' most of the time because the most frequent care-giver still tends to be the mother: but by the short-cut terms 'mother' and 'parent' we mean mother, father, foster-parent, nurse, house-parent or anyone else who is looking after the child in a 'mothering' way. In convenient contrast, we have used 'he' for both male and female 'professionals' in Chapter 10.

1 Development and handicap

When we talk of a child's *development*, what we usually mean is how he is progressing in a number of different areas – his movement, his speech, his thinking, his social behaviour and so on.

A 'normal' development involves the child learning about new things, learning new ways of doing things, and learning about people and how they behave. He also learns quite a lot about himself and how he fits into the world of things and people. Development usually follows naturally as a child grows bigger, stronger and more mobile, and as he makes contact with people and things around him.

No two children ever develop in an identical way. It would certainly be very convenient if all children progressed at a similar rate through all the different stages of development – and, broadly speaking, we *can* identify 'normal' types or stages of behaviour for different age-groups. But individual children have very different circumstances – they differ in health, surroundings, inherited abilities and their parents' ideas about how to bring them up. This means that some children progress more quickly than others, and that any one child makes more progress in some areas than in others.

WHAT DO WE MEAN BY A 'HANDICAPPED' PERSON?

'Handicap' can take many forms. It may be physical, or mental, or both. The world is not neatly divided up into 'normal' and 'handicapped' people. In most areas of life – physical, social, intellectual and so on – there are strong people and weak people. In ordinary language when we say someone is handicapped, all we really mean is that they are weak in a particular area – they may or may not be strong in other areas.

A particular handicap may be obvious at birth; or it may develop later; or it may have been present at birth but not noticeable until the baby gets old enough for us to see that he is not doing the things that we would expect a normal baby to do. It may or may not affect a child's physical appearance or

4

all his abilities. It may be inherited or the result of something going wrong during the pregnancy; or it may be caused by a particular event, such as illness or injury. It may have no explanation; many children are 'developmentally delayed' for reasons that we cannot discover. Luckily, we do not need to know the cause of a child's handicap in order to start helping him to learn.

It is also true to say that children with single well-defined handicaps are less common than they used to be, while children with several related handicaps make up a bigger proportion of handicapped children. This is partly because we are better at preventing some of the single handicaps which used to be caused by damage before or during birth, and partly because we are also better at keeping multi-handicapped children alive who at one time would have died at birth or in early childhood.

Simply to say that a child is 'handicapped' does not tell us very much about that child. If we think of development as consisting of a number of different areas, then what we really need to know is in which areas the child is progressing slowly. We can then try to work out why this might be, and suggest ways of improving things.

Sometimes it is easy to see why a child's difficulties are building up. For example, normal babies learn a lot about their world by 'exploring' it with their eyes; later on, they move around to examine things which attract them. If a child is blind, however, or cannot move around normally, then his opportunities to experience the world for himself are at once very limited. This is his real handicap, and we need to start thinking, as early as possible, about how to make up for it. The physically handicapped child will need all the help we can give him to organise his environment – that is, the people and things around him – in a way which will open up new experiences for him and allow him to develop as similarly as possible to the normal child, despite his physical limitations. In other cases, however, problems are harder to pinpoint and a lot of careful thought and imagination will be needed in order to help the child in the most effective way. This handbook is intended just to get us started in what for most people will be unknown territory.

THE BEGINNINGS OF LEARNING

As a starting point it may be useful to try and imagine what the daytime world is like for any little baby. It must be a very confusing, and sometimes frightening place, with lots of sound, light and movement seeming to rush past in a wild and uncontrolled way. Bit by bit, though, the infant learns that the world does have some *structure* – that is, some order and organisation – to it. He begins to be able to predict what will happen at certain times or during certain activities. He also begins to learn that what he says and does has results in what other people say and do back to him. The world *begins to make sense* to him.

1 Development and handicap

One of the things he learns about other people's reactions is that there are some things he does which they obviously don't like – they frown, or speak sharply, or maybe even tap his hand. With other things he does, they smile at him, or show they approve just by watching him without interfering. He begins to have some understanding of the 'structure' of his parents' approval: in other words, he can answer the question 'What do my parents approve of?', and he can predict in advance which behaviour they will consider 'good' and which they regard as 'naughty'.

For the mentally handicapped child, these various 'structures' may not have become clear. He may not be able to sort out what to expect of different things or different people. He may not understand how to communicate what he wants and how he feels. He may not make sense of what people try to communicate to him; and as a result of that, he may have difficulty in discovering how to behave 'acceptably'. In short, he doesn't know the 'rules of the game', and he doesn't know how to find them out either. So the world remains for him a confused, perhaps scaring place, and his behaviour reflects this: it may be wild and unpredictable, panicky and a little desperate, or perhaps withdrawn and cut off from reality – maybe all of them in turn.

Once again we need to try and change his environment to help him over this confusion. One of the aims of the so-called 'behavioural' approach to handicap, which we shall be concentrating on in this handbook, is to make it clearer to the child what his parents would like him to do, and what they can tolerate him doing, by keeping everything as plain and simple as possible for him. The things they would like him to do, of course, include the 'independent' things he'd like to do for himself, if only he could get as far as trying them out.

Most ordinary children seem to pick up their parents' feelings very easily, just as parents sense how their children are feeling. They learn very quickly how far they can go before their parents lose their tempers – even if sometimes they decide to push things just that little bit further! But mentally handicapped children, in particular, seem to find this understanding extraordinarily difficult. As a result, not only do they often ignore their parents' efforts to teach them new things (even play activities) – they also may push their parents so far that parents themselves become panicky and confused, and find themselves both worn out and at their wits' end about what to do. In short the child, through no fault of his own, is driving to distraction the people who most need to be calm and capable if they are to help him.

WHAT IS A BEHAVIOURAL APPROACH?

In a behavioural approach, instead of just assuming that things will somehow work out all right in the end so long as parents and children are fond of each other, we make the decision that special difficulties need specially organised thinking. We deliberately take a cool look at *behaviour* on both sides – child's and parent's (and, very important, anyone else who might be involved in the situation). We ask ourselves cool, hard questions. What *exactly* is the effect of my behaviour on the child? What *exactly* is the effect of his behaviour on me? (We've already seen that confused messages make a confused child, and a confused child confuses his parents.)

We don't just look at behaviour in general, which could muddle us even more. We divide up both our own behaviour and the child's into separate acts (which we can call 'behaviours') so that we can look at them more carefully and see their effects and their causes more clearly. Once we have an idea of the causes and effects of individual behaviours, we can begin to change our own behaviour to have a more helpful effect on the child. At that point, we hope that the child's own behaviour will change in response, and will have a less shattering effect on us. In this way, parents become more understandable to the child, child becomes more tolerable to parents, and each becomes more and more easy to live with – and more and more capable of coping with the world that faces each of us, child or adult.

The behavioural approach is one way of helping a handicapped child's development – and this applies both to his social development and to all his other capabilities. We need to know what the child can or cannot do, and to look for possible 'ways in' to development which will help us to work out how to change things to help him. There are extremely few children who are so severely handicapped that we cannot help them to make progress; and in fact we need to beware of *accepting* a child's problems by using the 'excuse' of handicap, whether it's an excuse for the child or an excuse for our own inaction. Instead of saying 'Oh, he can't manage that, poor thing, he's handicapped', we need to be saying, if it seems in any way possible, 'How can we change things so that he might learn to do that, or at least come close to it?'

There is always bound to be some uncertainty in the life of a handicapped child, and of those trying to help and support him. It is rare that we can predict how far a child is likely to develop in any particular area. Nevertheless we need to make sure that the child has the opportunity to progress as far as he can, and this handbook is designed to help us find ways of doing just that.

The next chapter will look a little more closely at a behavioural approach to child development. We will think about it as a method of communication – in this case, between parent and child. For parents whose chief worry is 'I don't seem able to get through to him', and whose second worry is 'I can't understand what he wants', communication seems the place to begin.

So what now?

Let's take some of the thoughts in Chapter 1 further, by looking at an example of what we shall need to do in order to apply these ideas to a particular child.

WE NEED TO BE EXACT IN OUR THINKING AND LANGUAGE

Something we all do at times is to describe events in dramatic ways, which don't always give much detail about what actually happened. For example, here's a parent's description of a child's temper tantrum.

> 'He had an awful temper tantrum this morning for no reason at all. I tried everything to quieten him down but nothing seemed to work.'

What do we learn about what went on from this description? Or, to put it another way, which words in the description do we need to know more about?

Here are some suggestions:

- 'awful' – Does this mean long-lasting? Unusual in some way? Intense? etc.

- 'temper tantrum' – This means different things to different people. What actually happened – glaring, swearing, kicking, screaming, head-banging, throwing? etc.

- 'for no reason at all' – This often means 'it surprised me'.
  That may be because we weren't attending to what the *child* was attending to just before he exploded into a tantrum. This is why we need to think back over *where* and *when* it happened, *who* was around, and *what* they were doing.
  With handicapped children we can often be surprised but we may still be able to find some explanation for behaviour, if we ask the right questions.

- 'I tried everything' – Everything?
  What was tried?
  In what order?
  What might the *child* have thought was meant by all this?
  Did these different things add up to a confused message?

- 'nothing seemed to work' – Is he still having the tantrum?

Somehow he *did* stop, and we need to look at what was going on at the end of the particular behaviour, even if our own intended attempts failed.

We will be looking at these types of question again in later chapters, but the example above shows us the kinds of cool, hard questions we will have to ask. This has to come before we can begin to plan for any change in our behaviour.

Sometimes people have filmed themselves with their handicapped child. When they came to look at the film, they realised that some of the things the child did were for reasons that were quite clear to see on the film, but which they hadn't noticed at the time. Obviously we can't film everything we do (although it's very useful to look at yourself and your child on video if you ever get the chance). Instead, we have to try very hard to sharpen our powers of observation – to try and look back at ourselves *as if* we were watching a film – otherwise we can waste a lot of time 'trying everything' and backing losers.

'NORMAL' DEVELOPMENT AND HANDICAP

As we have seen, children progress at different rates in different areas of behaviour. Even allowing for this, we can broadly describe 'normal' development – meaning that *most* children can do certain things *around* a particular age – and the checklist in Appendix 1 is a useful guide to how children usually develop. Have a look at it, and then try to answer the following general questions for your own child, to see if this can help to pin down your own areas of concern and the priorities for action.

- What are his greatest strengths or abilities?
- Which areas of development is he weak in?
- Will his weak areas affect development in other areas?
- What is the biggest problem for *you* in living with him?
- What is *his* biggest problem in developing normally?
- If he could tell you, what would *he* say his biggest problem was?

2 Getting through to a handicapped child: a behavioural approach

In this chapter we shall look in a more detailed way at the 'behavioural' method of looking at children's development. You may sometimes hear an approach like this called 'behaviour modification' or 'behaviour therapy'. We don't ourselves like those terms very much, because they make it sound as if one person is 'doing something' to another mainly to control them. Of course all parents do try to influence their children; but the point we are making is that parents and children influence *each other*, by communicating and negotiating with each other. This is what we are trying to make possible for the handicapped child. Obviously, because the parent is much more capable than the handicapped child, it is the parent who will have to take the lead in creating the possibility of communication. Finding ways of doing this is what this handbook is all about.

Perhaps we should be clear about two things before we begin. Firstly, a behavioural approach applies to *all behaviour*, not just to children and not just to the handicapped. We can think about our own behaviour in this way, and we will need to, if we are going to get a clear picture of what effects we have on each other. Secondly, it is simply an *approach*. By this we mean that it is a *way of looking* at things. In the field of handicap certainly many psychologists feel that it is the best and most useful way to cope with practical problems; but the main thing to remember is that it is only the best way so long as it *is* the most helpful; there is no *right* way. And because it is an approach, there are no simple answers which apply to every case, like following a recipe in a cookbook. Instead, we are trying to get across a general point of view for looking at situations and tackling them – thinking in a behavioural way.

WHAT LIES BEHIND A PARTICULAR BEHAVIOUR?

The starting point for the behavioural approach is the idea that we *learn* behaviour for a reason: it doesn't just happen. We learn that some sorts of

10

behaviour are *worthwhile* for us and others are not. Normally, if something has a pleasant result for us (praise, money, satisfaction and so on) we are likely to do it again when the opportunity arises. On the other hand, if something has an unpleasant result (pain, blame, loss etc.) we are likely to avoid it in the future if we can.

Of course this is nothing particularly new. Although they might not think of it in the way we have just described, the behavioural approach is what most teachers and parents are using every day when they praise or reward some sorts of behaviour, and punish or show disapproval of others. They hope that their approval or disapproval will be *seen by the child* as 'pleasant result' or 'unpleasant result'. They hope that in this way they are encouraging the 'good' behaviours and discouraging the 'bad' behaviours.

But with a handicapped child, the position is often more complicated. As we saw in the first chapter, many mentally handicapped children do not seem able to sort out what is acceptable behaviour and what is not acceptable, or to learn things easily. 'Normal' approval or disapproval often does not seem to work well enough with these children.

Let us look a little more closely at 'unacceptable' behaviour, taking a behavioural approach. That is, we must suppose that this behaviour is somehow *worthwhile* for the child, however odd this may seem to us, since he keeps on doing it. We may wonder what can be worthwhile about constant screaming, self-injury, or destroying things. The first thing we need to do is to sort out what might make it worthwhile *for this child*.

What do children value? Well, at an early age, we might suggest, children most value things like attention, their favourite food, or a cuddle. Later, things like music, a particular toy, or a word of praise, become equally valuable to them.

Most of us, as parents, naturally act in very confusing ways, which normal children surprisingly manage to make sense of. But for a handicapped child, making sense of confusing behaviour is a lot more difficult.

Imagine a typical household scene. A parent is trying to do the washing, or fix the car, but can't get down to it because the child is throwing a tantrum. To stop this, the parent shouts at the child, maybe even slaps him (both of which, odd though it may sound at first, involve offering the child *attention*), or perhaps gives him a sweet to calm him down. Now suppose the child is playing quietly; the parent turns away to get on with the job, relieved to get a moment's peace – and *ignores the child*. Suddenly the child starts to scream again . . .

Looking at that situation, we could say that the message which is being put across to the child is that 'bad' behaviour is worthwhile – it brings reward (attention, sweets etc.) – and 'good' behaviour is 'worth' nothing. What we should be trying to do is to change this message, so that the child understands that it is good or acceptable behaviour which is worthwhile for him, while bad behaviour has no future in it and is not worth the effort. *We will need to do this in as clear a way as possible, so that there can be no doubt in the child's mind as to what is expected of him, and so that the most interesting results come from acting acceptably.*

When we start observing our child carefully, we will find that it is possible to divide up his behaviours into certain groups. There are *positive* behaviours – that is, useful abilities which he has which we can hope to build on later; there are *negative* behaviours – that is, behaviours which are not helpful or acceptable and which we would like to get rid of; and there are 'in-between' behaviours which are a bit of both.

A good example of this last group is tantrums. The word 'tantrum', of course, means different things for different children (and parents). There is no doubt that in many cases tantrums are entirely 'negative' behaviour and might need to be reduced before the child can give his attention to anything else. What, though, if the *only* form of communication which a child has with his parents is by tantrum-like behaviour? In this case we would not want immediately to get rid of that behaviour since this would be to destroy the only communication between parent and child. We are trying through a behavioural approach to create *better* communication between parent and child, *in both directions.* So we would be hoping instead to *change the form* of the behaviour, to 'shape' it into something which both parent and child can use as more acceptable communication between them.

We might think that our particular child is so withdrawn or inactive that none of this can have much to do with him. In fact, though, if we start looking at him with these 'positives' and 'negatives' in mind, we are likely to begin to notice more variety in his behaviour than we even knew was there. This will help us a lot in developing his good points.

If we are going to bring about change in behaviour, it is very important that we should be able to describe that behaviour accurately – both the behaviour that exists now, and the behaviour that we are after. We shall come back to this in more detail in the next chapters, but we can think about it briefly now. Whether we are going to deal with unacceptable behaviours (throwing food, say) or teach a new skill (such as washing), we need to know *exactly* what goes into that behaviour.

Neither throwing food nor washing consists of one single action. Both are a *series of smaller actions* which we need to be able to sort out before we make our plans to deal with them. For example, to teach a child to wash we might well need to teach him separately the skills of pulling up sleeves, putting the plug in, running and stopping water, taking soap and so on. We would also have to make sure that it is clear to him just what is expected and what is going to be rewarding. We can do this by making *only the actions we want from him* worth his while. When he does do these actions, he finds he gets something he values, even if it's just a word of praise or a cuddle.

12

Similarly, before we can tackle food-throwing, we will need to ask ourselves some questions, and answer them in some detail. When and where does the food-throwing occur? What usually happens just beforehand? What does the child throw, and how (at somebody or just on to the floor)? What happens afterwards? As a result of sorting out in our own minds exactly what is going on when this behaviour takes place, we hope to learn more about precisely what it means to the child. What in particular is rewarding to him, apart from the fact that it gets our attention? All of this information will help us work out how to communicate our messages to the child in ways which are clear enough for him to use.

DEVELOPMENT, COMMUNICATION AND THE BEHAVIOURAL APPROACH

We can now bring together and sum up the points that have been made in the last two chapters.

Children who are *not* handicapped usually learn quickly to 'make sense' of what we say to them and how we treat them – even though most of us in everyday life behave inconsistently, change our minds, act according to mood, and generally give our children very confusing 'messages'. If we listen critically to what we say to children (as well as what we do), we find that much of it is what one researcher (who is also a mother) calls 'garbage' – things said without thought and without much meaning either. Yet, amazingly, ordinary children sort this out, and work out which are the important bits to attend to and which is the garbage. What is more, they learn to gather all sorts of *shades of feeling*, as well as other kinds of meaning, from the *way* we speak, our facial expression, our gesture and our body language, and this adds to their understanding of our messages.

Mentally handicapped children, and some physically handicapped ones too, find it very difficult to do all this. If they are to make any sense of our messages at all, we have to

(a)   simplify – well beyond what is natural for people talking to small children, and

(b)   make the most important bits of the message stand out for the child.

We do both these things by making sure that responding to the important bits is worthwhile and rewarding to the child – that is, we 'reinforce' the important bits. Our aim is firstly that the child should be in no doubt as to what we are trying to get over to him or what we want of him; secondly, our aim is to become more aware of how *we* are behaving so that we can alter our behaviour if he needs us to.

So the behavioural approach is not mainly a way of training children to be good or behave properly. It is much more a means of helping a child to understand what is required of him and what might be possible for him, and of helping parents to look more closely at their own behaviour towards him. Once he understands our messages better, he will not need to spend so much time doing the anxious or protesting things that he does now because he has found us so confusing – rocking, screaming, tantrums, withdrawing and so on. Instead he will spend more time 'receiving' us and perhaps trying to get through to us – so that eventually we shall be on our way to more normal communication patterns.

Getting through to a child using the behavioural approach is *not* normal communication, and to most parents it will rightly feel very unnatural at first. We use the approach because we expect it to become a *bridge* to more natural communication. If we were going to be limited to these methods for ever, our aims would be rather low-level – just to make the child more tolerable to live with. That in itself may be important for our own mental health.

In the end, though, we are looking towards a more natural and flexible kind of communication. We don't want our interaction with the child always to be guided by methods and rules – we want it to be two-way and free-flowing. We want to be able to give our child a hug just because we love him, without stopping to think whether we are rewarding unacceptable behaviour – even though we might find it useful to come back to the behavioural approach as a temporary measure in order to get the child over a particular hump. When we begin to be able to move on from the behavioural approach, we will have helped our child to be more of a complete person in his own right.

So what now?

Let's test out how you might use some of the ideas in Chapter 2, by looking at a few practical examples.

'WORTHWHILENESS'

It can often be very difficult to work out what can possibly be worthwhile for the child about some sorts of behaviour. Perhaps the easiest way to begin is by remembering two things:

(1)   It is the person *doing* an action who decides on how worthwhile it is to him – not the person watching it. In other words, to understand 'worthwhileness' we shall have to try and see the world through our child's eyes, not our own.

(2)   'Worthwhile' doesn't necessarily mean 'nice' or 'pleasant' – it may just be the best option open to him so far as the child can see. Which would you rather have – three months in prison or a £500 fine? This is the kind of choice which may be facing our child – what he does may seem 'worthwhile' to him only in the sense that anything else seems worse.

Here are a couple of situations which can sometimes face parents. Have a look at them, and try to work out what we might mean in these cases by describing the child's behaviour as 'worthwhile to him'.

- Six-year-old Martin won't mix with other children at school, and spends most of his time standing in a corner and rocking back and forth.
- Four-year-old Debbie, who is blind and retarded, seems to gain most pleasure from poking her fingers deep into the sockets of her eyes; as a result she often gets eye infections.

Here are some suggestions:
- *Martin's rocking* – Think about his alternative: mixing with other children. Is it worth his while to mix?

  Are the other children aggressive?

  Does he find it difficult to join in their play because of physical difficulties? Or because of social or communicating difficulties?

  Does he seem unaware of, or uninterested in other children?

  Rocking may be comforting or reassuring in the face of these problems, however boring it looks.
- *Debbie's eye-poking* – Debbie is in the dark, and she doesn't have very creative ideas. She can't see what there is to play with, and she bumps herself when she tries to explore. She'll need a lot of help to find anything

15

more interesting than the flashes of light she 'sees' when she pokes at her eyes. She's also not aware that poking leads to infections, because the infection doesn't *immediately* result.

It might be useful at this point to write down any behaviours which your child has which puzzle you as to how they can be worthwhile to him. What are his alternative choices, so far as he can tell? Would they offer him still less?

CONFUSING MESSAGES

Below are three examples of how easy it is to mix our messages to children, and how difficult it can be in some situations to act consistently. Two are real-life examples; the other is a cartoon which may ring bells for many of us. Have a look at them and ask yourself the following questions:

● What messages did the mother mean to give?
● What messages did she *actually* give?
● What pressures made the mother act as she did?
● What has the child learned?

Example A

Jamie's mother is knitting on the sofa; Jamie is playing with his toys on the rug. She's trying to follow a difficult bit in the pattern. Jamie waves his rattle and shows it to his mother; she says 'just a minute'. Jamie rolls a ball to his mother and smiles at her; she frowns and tries to make sense of the pattern. Jamie says 'muh!'; she turns away and rummages in her workbox for a tape-measure. Jamie grabs at the potted palm on the hearth and pulls it over; his mother leaps up, crying 'Oh my goodness, Jamie, what are you doing?' – and in a flurry of activity she picks up the palm, puts Jamie on the settee with a biscuit, fetches brush and dustpan to sweep up the spilt earth, tells Jamie what a bad boy he is, and in general makes life much more interesting for him than it was ten minutes ago . . .

Example B

Tracey, a seven-year-old Down's syndrome (mongol) girl, has picked up several swear-words – probably because swear-words are usually said forcefully, so they stand out for her. Her parents are trying very hard to ignore her when she swears and to give her lots of response for the other things she says, so that she will find it more boring to swear. As a result, she's nearly forgotten about swearing. However, they take her to a café for tea; the waitress is slow, and Tracey, impatient, asks loudly 'Where's my bloody tea?' Horrified reaction from everyone within ear-shot; and Tracey's parents, embarrassed by the disapproving stares, feel they have to scold Tracey so as not to seem too soft with her. Tracey sits there happily, delighted with the tremendous reaction she has produced . . .

Example C

Some comments

All these children got the wrong message because their mothers were being their natural inconsistent selves. Jamie's mother was busy with her knitting pattern until he made her attend to him by causing a crisis that she couldn't ignore – she probably vaguely hoped that he was learning to be patient, but he'd have learned that better if she'd given him a quick encouraging smile when he showed her things. He may now have learned to pull the pot-plant over first instead of last!

Willy and Tracey have learned how useful crying and swearing can be, and especially they have both discovered that their parents can be 'got at' best in public. Tracey's parents were doing fine with the swearing problem until they found themselves under pressure from onlookers who didn't under-stand the situation. Willy's mother would probably have been more consis-tent without an audience. Most of us find it difficult to behave consistently when we are busy or distracted, flustered or embarrassed. With a handi-capped child, we may have to learn two different and difficult things – to be sensitive to the child's needs, but to develop a thick skin as far as other people's remarks are concerned.

BREAKING ACTIVITIES DOWN INTO STEPS

We will go into this in more detail in Chapters 5 and 6. For now, take the fol-lowing two teaching situations, and try to break them down into a series of small steps:

(A)   teaching a child to pick up a cup from a table and drink
(B)   teaching a child to put on knee-length socks

If we are aware of how many different things a child has to do in order to complete a task like this, we will become

- better at understanding which are the most difficult bits, and finding ways of helping him through them
- better at giving him encouragement at the right moments
- better at knowing what skills he needs *before* he can tackle an activity – for instance, for both these tasks the child must be able to grip and move the hands at the same time.

Some suggestions

Example A   Picking up a cup and drinking

(1)   Look at the cup.
(2)   Reach for the cup and grip it properly (with either one or two hands).
(3)   Lift the cup up, without tipping it.
(4)   Draw it carefully towards face.

18

(5)   Steady cup against bottom lip.
(6)   Tip cup slightly, mouth open.
(7)   Close mouth on liquid.
(8)   Swallow.
        (If the child is a 'thrower' you may want to add the step of returning the cup safely to the table!)

Example B   Putting on knee-length socks
(1)   Get in comfortable well-balanced position (sitting down).
(2)   Look at sock.
(3)   Pick up sock correctly (two hands, thumbs inside sock).
(4)   Bend down.
(5)   Lift toe up off floor.
(6)   Pull sock over toes.
(7)   Lift foot.
(8)   Pull sock over heels, pointing toes downwards.
(9)   Pull right up (and lower leg).
(10)   Turn down top – but this is too difficult to put in programme to start with.

(At an early stage in teaching, lay out the socks rolled down so that the foot can enter directly. Later, insert an extra step for getting the sock the right way round before (4).)

3 Looking at behaviour: choosing priorities

A parent (or whoever is acting as parent) is the only real expert on his or her child's behaviour. There is no-one who knows more about a child than the person who lives with him day in, day out. Of course, a lot of this knowledge is 'hidden'; that is to say, we might not be aware that we do know something until someone asks us the right question. One of the most important jobs which 'professionals' (doctors, teachers, psychologists, social workers and so on) have to do is to ask the right questions of the people who have the answers; and those people are very often the parents. The answers can then be used to work out what will best help the child.

Parents of handicapped children should not feel they are on their own in dealing with their child. Ideally they should be regularly supported and advised by a team of specialists in the different fields which might be involved in handicap (the professionals we've mentioned above, the various therapists, parent groups etc.). These people can offer the experience of having seen many different children with similar kinds of problems. For all that, it is still a child's parents who are the real experts on *this particular* child, and they should try to resist the natural feeling that they are the ignorant ones just because they are seeking advice. This handbook is intended to make us think about the kind of questions we should be asking ourselves and each other. In this way we will use to the full the knowledge *which we already have at our disposal*, simply from living with our child.

The first step in forming a plan for a particular handicapped child is to sort out exactly what the child can and cannot do. Sometimes it may be clear from what a parent has seen that a child is capable of a particular thing. At other times, we may be much less sure whether he can do it or not, and we may need to test this out more carefully. We may be able to do this by observing the child in his ordinary activities, but taking special care, so that we can be sure of what we are seeing – if he comes to table at the call 'Dinner's ready', did he really understand the words, or did he see and smell the dinner?

Sometimes the easiest way of finding out about some abilities is to use a test

20

designed for the purpose. When paediatricians, psychologists and therapists use tests, they are simply using a short-cut method to assess what a child *can* do, and what he has difficulty with, in order to suggest the next steps forward. This is something we have to know if we are to plan ahead properly. Professionals use tests mainly because they don't often have the opportunity to make careful observations over a long period of time. This is where parents who have learned how to observe accurately have an advantage over professionals.

Once we have an overall picture of a child's abilities in all the different areas which make up what we call 'development', we shall have some idea of the things which he is doing 'normally' for his age, and where he is progressing slowly. And if we keep a regular check on all the areas we tested to start with, we will be able to see the *rate* at which he is progressing, and what are the areas in which he will need extra help.

At this point, we shall also need to know from specialists whether there is any medical or physical reason which is going to make development in a particular area difficult, or perhaps impossible. This would apply particularly, of course, to physical handicaps.

We have emphasised the need to work out a reasonably clear picture of the child at the start, because if our ideas about him are muddled we cannot set up a really useful plan of action.

Most people find it helpful at this stage to make out a kind of 'balance sheet' for the child. This enables us to sort out the positive, the negative and the in-between aspects of the child which were mentioned in the last chapter: the plus and minus aspects of his behaviour. It will also be useful to have a fourth section for 'urgent needs'. Drawing up this kind of four-part list helps us to see how the child's needs fit together and where we should start.

What kind of things are we going to put in our four sections?

'POSITIVE BEHAVIOURS'

Here we will list abilities or characteristics or skills the child now has, and particularly those on which we might build in teaching him something new. For instance, if he likes being praised, or concentrates longest on toys that are shiny, or smiles at musical sounds, these are characteristics that will be useful to us in helping to work out teaching activities which he is likely to find interesting. Having a list of his skills also reminds us not to take them for granted, but to show appreciation of them to the child from time to time, so that he does not let go of them.

'NEGATIVE BEHAVIOURS'

Here we will write down behaviour which is definitely dangerous, or antisocial behaviour which is a real nuisance, or behaviour which is definitely preventing his progress. For instance, if he has an urge to break windows, hit

21

the baby or throw flower pots, these are all behaviours which we would like to get rid of fast. If he screams whenever he's bathed, this is not dangerous but it is a nuisance. If he insists on holding a cotton reel in each clenched fist, this will prevent him exploring objects with his fingers and get in the way of his learning new things.

We may also write down here any behaviour which is not too bad in itself but which is causing a lot of stress to his parents. For instance, some parents get very upset if a child comes in their bed at night, while others don't mind. If a behaviour is really making a parent feel desperate, it is worth putting it down in the 'negative' column and trying to do something about it. Desperate parents don't do the child any good; he needs people who are feeling reasonably calm.

'IN-BETWEEN BEHAVIOURS'

It is worthwhile adding this middle column because there are some behaviours which are just that – somewhere between positive and negative. For instance, the child may show behaviour which is *almost* positive – he feeds himself quite well but smears the food all over his face; or he loves his bath but drinks so much of it that his bed is soaked every night. These are things that just need a little 'shaping up' to make them real positives, and it's worth making a note of them. There are also behaviours which have both positive and negative aspects – for example, the tantrums we met in the last chapter are at least a form of communication, though a rather poor one. Here again, we need to shape the tantrum into a more acceptable form of communication.

'URGENT NEEDS'

Under this heading, we put those problems in the child's behaviour which we shall have to solve in order to make any progress. These vary according to the stage of development.

For instance, as soon as possible the child needs to respond to his own name, look at his mother when she speaks to him, and keep still and listen for a few seconds, if he is going to learn from her. Later, he needs to make sounds before he can be helped to shape them into words. Similarly, he must be aware when he's urinating before he can choose to urinate in the right place. These 'urgent needs' reminds us what the *first* steps are in learning, speaking, toilet-training – or in later skills like reading and arithmetic, for that matter.

22

So our final balance sheet will look something like this:

	Positive behaviours	In-between behaviours	Negative behaviours
URGENT NEEDS			

CHOOSING PRIORITIES

We have now set out our information clearly enough to be able to choose *priorities for action*: what is most urgent for the child's development, or to protect him and others from danger, or to make him easier to live with. *We cannot expect everything at once*, any more than a normal child does all his learning at the same time. So we select the behaviour which we most need to change or perhaps to introduce. This might be to teach the child something new, or to stop him behaving in a particular unacceptable way, or to 'shape' an existing behaviour differently. We must be precise about what our aim is; we must base what we do on accurate observation; and on the whole we must concentrate our teaching efforts on a little at a time.

If we are trying to introduce a behaviour or a skill which a child does not have at the moment, we first need to be clear in our minds about all the individual parts which make up the behaviour. We have to work out the separate steps which will eventually add up to his achieving the skill, and at first we will reward each step in order that the child will understand that each step is worth his while. (It is difficult for him to look ahead and see how the steps are going to add up, so we have to give him separate clear messages.) Eventually we shall be rewarding him for putting the steps together in the right order, and finally we look forward to him experiencing the success of carrying through the whole sequence.

In shaping up an in-between behaviour, we have the advantage of being able to build on a skill or ability which is already partly there. We need to think carefully about what small items of behaviour make up what the child does now, and then separate them into those we want to keep because they would also be part of the better behaviour we're aiming at, and those which now get in the way of that better behaviour. We can then do two things: firstly, we can deliberately reward the 'good bits' and refuse to give attention for the 'bad bits'; secondly, in our reaction to the behaviour as a whole, we can gradually step up the standard of behaviour which we will reward, so that we steadily increase our expectations in time with the child's gradual improvement.

23

3   Looking at behaviour: choosing priorities

If we are trying to reduce or stop a certain behaviour, we must do two basic things. Firstly, we must be clear when and where the behaviour happens, and what *exactly* goes on just before, during and afterwards. This involves watching not only what the child does but also what *we ourselves* are usually doing at the time, especially in relation to him. Secondly, we must try and guess what might be making the behaviour worthwhile for the child, and then deliberately try to alter things, so that the child clearly gets the message that this particular behaviour is *not worthwhile for him*. At the same time we may need to make clear the kind of behaviour we do want in the particular situation, again by making it obvious to the child that the 'correct' behaviour *is* worthwhile for him.

Don't forget that the 'reward' which we will need to give a child to show him that we want him to behave in a certain way will be different from child to child and from situation to situation: this is discussed in Chapter 5.

Sometimes we find that whatever we have planned feels fairly natural to us, at other times it may feel rather 'stiff' and unnatural; but we must always remember that we are trying to *communicate a message clearly* to a child who has difficulty understanding 'ordinary' communication. Sometimes it may require a lot of repetition on our part, but we must be sure that we are consistent in the message we are putting across, so that he can understand what his bchaviour means for us.

To sum up then: in this chapter we have tried to make three main points. Firstly, we must from the start have a full picture of a child's abilities and particular difficulties. Secondly, this will help us to make a balance sheet showing how his characteristics help or prevent future progress, and the balance sheet will enable us to work out our priorities sensibly. Thirdly, having selected a particular behaviour we hope to change or introduce, we need to go into that behaviour in a lot of detail, to be sure in our own minds of the message we are trying to put across to the child, and to work out how, when and where we can put it across most effectively.

In the next two chapters we will look in more detail into the questions of *how* we observe a child's behaviour, and how we can best manage the business of rewarding in order to make our messages really clear.

So what now?

How do we set about drawing up a balance sheet and deciding which needs are most urgent?

In drawing up a balance sheet, it will help if we compare our everyday knowledge of our child with a development checklist such as the one in Appendix 1. This gives us an idea of the order in which development usually happens, so we can see where our own child has got to, and what is likely to happen next. Using a developmental checklist tells us what is sensible to aim for and what we shouldn't expect for a while yet.

Positive behaviours are those characteristics and skills which a child *now* has, which we can build on; *negative* behaviours are the ones that prevent his progress or create stress for the family; and *in-between* behaviours have both good and bad points, so that we would want to change them just a bit to make them more positive with less negatives mixed in.

Sorting out behaviours in this way can take some time, and you may feel that you'd rather be getting on with teaching your child. It's worth doing, though, because it does help us to think in the cool, clear way we will need to if we are to plan the programme properly and make it work.

Here's an example of what your first balance sheet might look like. This one is quite short – as John's parents went on thinking about it, they added more things. Then it was even more important to decide which things to work on first.

Child: **John**   Age: **5**

Positive behaviours	In-between behaviours	Negative behaviours
Smiles when verbally praised	Only concentrates on toys for a few minutes then throws them	In and out of bed all evening
Can feed himself with fingers	Says 'wee', then wets pants	Kicks adults and children in frustration
Can thread three pieces on to pile-up toy	Carries big teddy about all the time	Spits food on table
Undresses himself; pulls pants up, puts socks on		Won't sit down except for meals
Likes rough and tumble play		
Says six words: mummy, dad, no, cup, choccy, wee		

URGENT NEEDS	Sitting down – increasing concentration

25

3   Looking at behaviour: choosing priorities

What was in John's parents' minds as they made out this balance sheet? Something like this:

POSITIVE BEHAVIOURS

Smiles when verbally praised

'He does seem pleased when we say "You are clever, John" or "Good boy". He really loves us to say "Hooray for John" and he's got a special thing about "Fantastic!" So we can use all those to reward him, and keep "Fantastic!" for the really big moments.'

Can feed himself with fingers

'Well, that's something anyway. We can let him keep finger-feeding for dry food, but if he wants the mushy food he'll have to use the spoon himself – we've got to stop spoon-feeding him just for speed. Luckily he does like his jelly and custard, *and* mashed potato, so he'll be keen.' (You'll find some ideas that John's parents used on pages 56–9.)

Can thread three pieces on to pile-up toy

'Come to think of it, that shows he should be able to use a spoon too, if he tries! We'd like him to get a bit further with a toy – he seems to get bored fast. Perhaps that toy *is* boring? If only he'd put that bit more effort in, toys would be more rewarding to him, and he'd enjoy himself more instead of getting frustrated.'

Loves bath

'Yes, he's really happy then. Relaxed, too. Perhaps he'd concentrate better in the bath – aren't there some toys we could use with him then?
* We ought to give him more attention then, anyway, because he seems to respond best in the bath – we always seem to use that time for sorting the dirty clothes . . . could be a waste of good play-time for us and John together!'

Undresses himself; pulls pants up

'Well, we know undressing is easier than dressing, but maybe that bath has something to do with it too! It would be nice if we could make it worth his while to dress himself. He'd be pleased as well – if he could only concentrate long enough. Again, we dress him ourselves just for speed, but surely he could do *some* of it.' (Some ideas for this are on pages 53–4.)

Likes rough and tumble play

'That's the easiest way to feel close to John, and he does love it and seems more affectionate. We'll carry on with that, but it'd be nice if we could find a quiet way to be close as well. Work on bathtime? If only he'd concen-

26

trate on toys – other children play with their parents like that. Perhaps other kinds of "play" might help – digging? cooking? music? washing-up?' (There are ideas for this on the pages following Chapters 7 and 8.)

Says six words

'You can do a lot with six words, and of course there are other ones he just understands. He does need more, ones that would be useful to him, and we could work on that. We'd like him to say "Yes" as well as "No"! More words first, then putting two together perhaps. If he'd concentrate, we could look at picture books and lotto cards.'

IN-BETWEEN BEHAVIOURS

Only concentrates on toys for few minutes, then throws them

'Well he does at least last a few minutes! But the throwing's a nuisance. If he didn't throw, we could get him nicer toys maybe – at the moment things break so quickly. He never seems to get stuck in to a toy – never even sits down to it, so how does he know what's in it for him?'

Says 'wee', then wets pants

'Full marks for saying "wee" – and at the right time, too. That must mean he knows it's coming. But then he doesn't wait long enough. Either he needs to realise it earlier, or he needs to hold it longer once he's realised. Perhaps we could get better organised too, so he gets the *habit* of getting it in the potty, not down his legs. And it's got to be more worthwhile to *him* to get it in the potty!'

Carries teddy about all the time

'It's nice to see him doing that, and his teddy's a big comfort to him – BUT he never lets go of it. So his arms are always full of teddy and therefore it's hard for him to pick up toys or anything else. He does seem to be missing out on play in that way. We thought we might start by giving him a teddy about half the size, so he can tuck it under his arm and use his hands for other things. Then (let's hope!) he might get more interested in playing with toys and *want* to put the teddy down where he can see it. We thought that at that point we might pin a tiny teddy – one of those 3-inch ones – on to his jumper, so that he can accept being moved away from the bigger one; that would really make him much more free to play.'

3 Looking at behaviour: choosing priorities

NEGATIVE BEHAVIOURS

In and out of bed all evening

'This one's for us! We really need a bit of peace at the end of a day with John. At the moment he gets a lot of fun out of coming down and getting taken up again, with all the bribes of "one more song" and drinks of water and so on. We've decided we don't really mind him getting out of bed so long as he doesn't come down. So we'll start by putting really warm nightclothes on him, so we don't have to worry about him getting cold. Then we'll make sure that the things he likes are in the bedroom, and a small light on. Then we'll try to make it less worthwhile for him to come down – take him up again very quickly without having a chat and without any bribes – somehow it's got to be more worthwhile to stay in his bedroom than come downstairs. We'll give that a fair try, but if it doesn't work we thought we might put a catch on the door to show him we mean it – if we do have to do that, we'll borrow a two-way baby alarm from the toy library, so that we can hear what he's doing and so that we can talk to him soothingly. Our friends have got a handicapped child they just let stay up all evening, and that's fine because they're happy about it – but we get very stroppy if we don't get some time to ourselves, and that can't be good for John, so we're going to hold out on this one.'

Kicks adults and children in frustration

'No-one likes having bruises on their legs – and we're losing friends fast! We're hoping we might be able to cut down the frustration once we look carefully at the situations where he gets frustrated. Also, if we can learn to sense the kick coming we might prevent it – maybe just hold him firmly and love him. If he does kick, we're going to try to hold back on the big reaction – perhaps just put him outside the room for half a minute, without any fuss. But we're pretty sure prevention is the thing to go for if we can.'

Spits food on table

'We *know* he does this for the attention, and he certainly succeeds in getting it. Luckily he likes his food, so he needs to learn that food and spitting don't go together. We'll try removing his plate right out of sight and out of reach when he spits on the table – for one minute the first time he spits, for good if he does it again in the same meal. This is something he'll probably learn quite quickly, though he might come back to it to see if we still mean it. We thought we'd keep this to spitting *on the table* – he's got to be able to spit out something he really hates, so if he spits it on to his plate we'll just ignore that. We can't expect *too* much at a time!'

28

3 Looking at behaviour: choosing priorities

Won't sit down except for meals

'Here again, he's missing out on all the toys that need a bit of concentration. There are two things we might try to start with. Since he does sit down at meals, we'll have a five-minute play session at the table at the end of every meal – the washing up can wait that long! He usually finishes up with a bit of apple or a rusk, so we could start showing him a toy while he's still eating that. On top of that, we'll have regular play sessions where he gets rewarded just for sitting and looking when we ask him – five minutes at first, we thought. We're hoping that he'll soon think it's worth his while to stick at it for longer, because he'll realise we've got interesting things to show him if he sits down and looks.' (See pages 43–4 for a description of this kind of session.)

URGENT NEEDS

'Looking at all these things, it seems as if concentration comes into an awful lot of them. If we could get him to sit and look for a few minutes, a lot of other things would follow. So we'll start with that, and perhaps the teddy business as well, because he needs free hands to *use* that concentration. We did think of putting in this "coming downstairs in the evening" as something that urgently needs dealing with – because it does seem to get under our skin and makes us feel really under pressure. We might think about that – but it's possible that concentrating more in the day will tire him out and make him sleep better anyway, so it could cure itself. Also, we'll be giving him lots more attention when we're teaching him to concentrate, so he may not feel he needs it so much in the evening. It looks as if helping him to concentrate will make the other programmes easier, maybe even unnecessary. Here's hoping, anyway!'

TO SUM UP:

If you look back at the starred sentences, you'll see that there are already quite a lot of practical ideas which could be included in a programme to improve John's concentration. In fact, by the time John's parents had worked through these thoughts, they were already a long way towards having a programme which was likely to succeed.

You'll notice that for one of the 'negative' behaviours, spitting food on the table, John's parents did not regard *all* spitting as 'negative': they were prepared to let him spit out food on his plate if he didn't like it. It does quite often happen that certain behaviour is only really objectionable because of the time and place the child chooses. For instance, most parents know and accept that children masturbate (play with their genitals) in bed or in other private places, though they may feel upset if the child insists on displaying

29

this in public. Handicapped children may do this more than other children, if only because they have fewer interesting things to do; and parents often ask how to stop them. It is usually much more effective to concentrate on making the child understand when and where he *may* do this, rather than trying to stop him altogether, which most people wouldn't attempt with a normal child.

In sorting out your own thoughts, it might be helpful to ask yourself the following questions:

- What new behaviour would be most useful to my child? Why?
- What behaviour he has now would it be most useful *to him* to change? Why?
- What new behaviour in my child would be most helpful to *me* in coping with him? Why?
- Which of his present behaviours do I most need to change, for my own sake? Why?
- Taking these all together, the area of most urgent need for us as a family is . . . What?
- Is there anything that would make it difficult to start with this? What can we do about that?

4 Looking at behaviour: making it work

In this chapter we will look more closely at our reasons for making notes about a child's behaviour before planning how to teach him. In the next, we shall look at how we teach him that certain behaviour is worthwhile.

OBSERVING AND RECORDING BEHAVIOUR

It is difficult to get to know enough about a behaviour we are trying to change, unless we make some kind of record as to what is going on. The same thing will be true when we try to see what effect our teaching is having.

The form of record we choose to make is very much up to us as individuals, and it also depends on the type of behaviour involved. Suppose we are trying to stop a particular behaviour. If the behaviour seems to happen unpredictably at various times during the day, we would want to record the number of times it happened, where and when this was, what happened before, during and after, and what we ourselves were doing at the time. On the other hand, if a behaviour only happens at certain regular times of day (e.g. mealtime, night-time), then obviously we would want to keep our recording to those times of day when the behaviour takes place.

Basically, we need to know how frequent the behaviour is and the circumstances in which it occurs (when, where, what happens and what we were doing both before and afterwards). This does not mean that we have to write pages and pages every day; often a simple chart will do, and we can use ticks and crosses to save writing. The main thing is that we don't leave anything out which might help us in explaining the behaviour.

It is very important that we try to improve on our usual vague ways of describing behaviour. If we are to be as precise as we need to be, expressions like 'he's aggressive' or 'he spends all day screaming' aren't much help to us. What one person means by 'aggressive' is not a description of behaviour, but more the meaning someone *reads into* that behaviour.

What we need to know is exactly *how* the child behaves. Does he kick, scratch, punch or what? What or whom does he do it to? What happens

31

beforehand? In what circumstances does he quieten down? – and so on Similarly 'all day' rarely means 'all day long'. We need to know *how often* and for *how long* the behaviour occurs, what was the order of events, and whether there is a regular pattern (is it worst in the mornings, afternoons or evenings, before or after meals, when certain people are present, or when?).

What we are trying to do is to collect enough information to be able to reorganise and *manage* the situation. For instance, sometimes we may find that a particular behaviour only actually happens in a particular place: and simply by moving the child to a different place we can achieve some improvement.

The same sort of rules apply if we want to introduce a new skill. Perhaps the child can do what we want him to sometimes, but not all the time. Again we need to know the circumstances he seems to need for this to happen.

If we work out the individual steps which go to make up a skill or behaviour that we want, we may then find that the child can already manage some of these steps. Maybe he just needs to learn one or two more steps, or perhaps his difficulty is in bringing the steps together in the right sequence. Either way, we need to know which of the child's behaviours we can build on, and how and when they are produced.

THE TEACHING PROGRAMME

At this stage, we shall be ready to work out our teaching plan, using the ideas on 'rewards' and 'non-rewards' in the next chapter. We have now identified precisely which bit of behaviour needs to be changed in order to make progress in the most helpful way. We have looked at the behaviour *as it is now*, compared with the behaviour *as we want it to be*. And we have thought carefully about what seems to make the old behaviour happen (what makes it worthwhile), and what might make the new behaviour take its place (how we can make that *more* worthwhile). We have been able to think about this constructively because we have made accurate observations of the situation instead of just letting ourselves get upset about the problem. Now we can plan in an informed way. And the teaching plan really only consists of the answers to two questions:
(1)   How can I help the child to understand what I want him to do?
(2)   How can I make this new behaviour more attractive to him than the old behaviour?

The information we have gathered should give us at least *some* kind of answer to each of these questions – enough of an answer to try out.

While we are trying out our teaching plan, we must of course go on making observational records in just the same form and at the same times, because we need to get a clear idea of what effect our teaching is having. We may feel as if we already have a much better understanding with our child even when his behaviour hasn't actually improved. That's important, but we do want actual improvement as well. So we must continue to keep notes so that we can check just how successful the plan is. Again, the child may be very slow in his response, and we can easily feel disappointed until, by checking our records over time, we find that he is actually making slow but steady progress.

It is always difficult to predict results. The better we do our homework – that is, our careful and precise observations – the more likely we are to achieve positive results. Sometimes this may happen very quickly and surprise us; at other times it may seem to go on and on. Either way, good record-keeping will show us (depending on what we are trying to do) whether a certain behaviour is on the decrease, whether the child is progressing along the steps we have set out for him, and so on.

In the early days, perhaps it is best not to set our sights too high, but to choose a problem which is fairly clear-cut. After all, we are feeling our way at this stage, and learning a new approach to the child. We are not yet used to working with him in this way, and nor is he. With a straightforward problem, we are more likely to be successful; and a feeling of achievement is what we all need in order to go on to more complicated problems with confidence.

It may also be worthwhile to set ourselves a time-limit – perhaps a fortnight – after which we will look at our progress and perhaps decide to change some part of the teaching plan if things are not working out well. (If real difficulties are arising out of the plan, of course, there is nothing to stop us changing it earlier than this.)

If the plan is not working at all, we must be prepared to admit this. At the same time, we need to ask ourselves one or two direct questions. Did we actually carry out the programme as we planned it? How did the child understand our message, and could he in fact have received a confused message? Rather than get disheartened, we need to try and see things through the child's eyes; what did the situation look like *to him*? Then we may either tighten up the way we are carrying out the plan or perhaps change it slightly in the light of what we have learned.

Often parents feel that it will be boring and a lot of work making notes in this way. Sometimes they feel that this is the kind of thing they didn't much enjoy at school and they don't really want to go back to it. Obviously there *is* a certain amount of work involved. On the other hand, it does make the teaching plan much more likely to be successful; and it's not nearly so much work as going on coping with the difficult behaviour for the next few years.

So what now?

Chapter 4 has been intended to start us thinking about how we can get a *more accurate picture* of behaviour which we want to improve or change in some way. How to go about the actual task of changing the behaviour will be tackled in Chapter 5. For now, let's concentrate on how to measure the way he behaves *now*, and how to check whether we and our child are making progress once we have begun our programme.

There are four important questions we will need to think about carefully before starting our recording:

(1) How do I describe clearly the behaviour I need to change?
(2) When and for how long am I going to do this recording?
(3) How should I go about recording the behaviour which I've described, to check what's going on?
(4) What do I do with all this information once I've got it?

(1) HOW DO I DESCRIBE CLEARLY THE BEHAVIOUR I NEED TO CHANGE?

In the 'So what now?' section of Chapter 1, we looked at the vague ways people often use to describe behaviour. We must be sure that our description would make it crystal clear *to another person* what our child is doing. As we saw in Chapter 1, the kinds of words we need to use are words which describe the *behaviour itself*. The kinds of words we need to avoid are those which are just our *opinion* of the behaviour (such as 'good', 'bad-tempered', 'naughty'). We may first have to look much more closely at our child's behaviour, before we can arrive at a clear enough description to begin our recording.

Have a look at the descriptions below and see which you think are *clear* and which are *unclear*. There are three of each.

- 'Sarah eats really messily.'
- 'Simon threw his cup across the room six times this morning.'
- 'Michael cries for half an hour when he is put to bed.'
- 'Caroline has tantrums at the slightest thing.'
- 'Paula can feed herself with a spoon, using either hand.'
- 'Billy is always trying to get attention.'

For the three *unclear* ones (Sarah, Caroline and Billy), what questions would you ask the person speaking so as to get a more accurate picture of the behaviour?

Once we have arrived at a description of the behaviour, it's a good idea to jot it down on our records so that we – and others – are sure *what counts as the behaviour* when we are recording it. Our description may be simple ('smiling'), limited in time ('eye-contact – looking us in the eye – for two seconds'), or a pattern of behaviour ('lying on floor, kicking legs and screaming').

(2) WHEN AND FOR HOW LONG AM I GOING TO DO THIS RECORDING?

There is no single answer to this; it's mainly a matter of common sense. We don't want to be running round all day with sheets of paper in our hands, furiously writing notes. On the other hand, we do need enough information to be pretty sure about what is happening *now*, and what effect our programme has once it starts. This is why, whatever we write down, we would normally want to record our child's behaviour for a week or so *before* starting our programme, and go on until it is obvious that we have got the improvement we want. This way, in the early stages we shall probably discover things which will help us plan our programme better; and later on, we shall have a clearer idea of exactly what changes are happening as a result of the programme, even before they are obvious.

(3) HOW SHOULD I GO ABOUT RECORDING THE BEHAVIOUR WHICH I'VE DESCRIBED, TO CHECK WHAT'S GOING ON?

Again, there are no hard-and-fast rules about this: choose whichever method fits any individual case. Remember, you won't be using all these ways each time.

In most cases we will need to find a way of noting *where* the behaviour happened and *who* was there when it happened, so that we can find out if particular people, particular places or particular situations are affecting the behaviour. If we suspect that people or places are important in setting off problem behaviour, what we plan will have to take account of this. As well as what seemed to *trigger* the behaviour, we need to make a note of what seemed to *stop* it, as this, too, will help us plan ahead.

From what we already know about the behaviour, we will have some idea whether we're mainly interested in *how often* the behaviour occurs or *how long* it lasts. For example, if the behaviour we're trying to measure is sitting and concentrating on a particular toy, what we want to know is how long our child can now manage to do this. If, on the other hand, the behaviour is something like throwing objects or shouting swear-words, it would be more useful to know how often this is happening. Some other kinds of behaviour – for instance eye-contact, screaming bouts or playing with another child – are less easy to put in one or the other category; we might want to record both how often and for how long this kind of behaviour happens.

Summing up: to record behaviour we must first ask ourselves:

- Do I want to know *how often* the behaviour occurs, *how long* it goes on for, or both?

- Do I need to check on the *places* where the behaviour occurs?
- Do I need to check on *who is around* when the behaviour occurs?
- Do I need to check on the *triggers* for the behaviour – what sets it off?
- Do I need to note why the behaviour seemed to stop when it did – that is, what happened *just before it stopped*?

Let's see how these records of 'how often' and 'how long' work out in practice.

'HOW OFTEN' RECORDS

Here we want to record the *frequency* of the behaviour – *how often* it happens. This behaviour may be:

- very frequent throughout the day
- very infrequent
- erratic so far as we can see – we're looking for a pattern.

Very frequent behaviour. It would be exhausting, and probably unnecessary, to record every example during the day. It is more reasonable to record the behaviour at, say, three or four stages during the day for a certain period of time – an hour, twenty minutes, or even ten minutes, depending on the behaviour. Remember that our main aim is to get a picture of the *typical* frequency of the behaviour. We are taking *samples of time* in order to find this out.

We could then draw up a recording chart something like the one below, and simply tick off the number of times we observe the behaviour we have described in Question (1).

Example A

Monday		Simon throws crockery or hard objects				
Time sample		Trigger	Place	People	Why stopped	Total
8–9 a.m.	✓	Gave him juice	Kitchen	All 5 family	Nothing left to throw	3
	✓	Said 'eat your cereal'	Kitchen	All except Daddy	Fed him	
	✓	Picked up baby	Kitchen	Mother	Don't know	
2–3 p.m.	✓	Don't know	Supermarket	Lots of customers	Smacked, took out	1
6–7 p.m.	✓	Baby into bath	Bathroom	Mother, baby	Put S in bath	2
	✓	Took S out of bath	Bathroom	Mother	Cuddled	

36

Infrequent or erratic behaviour. Here we are more likely to want to record throughout the day, to see if any patterns emerge. Making records can often surprise both parents and professionals. It can help them to see that behaviour which they thought was random or inconsistent actually had a pattern to it – and that makes it easier to see how to deal with it. Here's an example of an all-day chart for recording frequency of behaviour. In this case, Caroline's mother felt that Caroline had more tantrums with her than with anyone else, so she added a record of what she herself was doing at the time, in order to check whether she was somehow provoking Caroline's tantrums.

Example B

Monday						Caroline flings herself on floor screaming											
a.m.6	7	8	9	10	11	p.m.12	1	2	3	4	5	6	7	8	9	10	11
		✓	✓		✓	✓	✓					✓	✓				
			✓			✓	✓						✓				
			✓			✓	✓						✓				
						✓	✓										
						✓	✓										

| Total | | 1 | 3 | | 1 | 5 | 5 | | | | | 1 | 3 | | | | |

Mother attending to Caroline	Mother attending to baby	Mother attending to Father	Mother doing housework	Mother not there
✓	✓ ✓ ✓ ✓ ✓ ✓ ✓ ✓ ✓	✓ ✓ ✓ ✓ ✓	✓ ✓ ✓	✓

Day's total: 19

By looking at a week's totals for particular hours in the day, and thinking about what goes on in the household during these times, we will get a clear picture of how consistent our child's behaviour is, and what we might do to improve things.

'HOW LONG' RECORDS

To record the *duration* of a behaviour (*how long* it occurs), we shall obviously need a watch or clock – a second hand is useful. As with 'how often' records, we will need to decide whether we wish to time *every occurrence* of the behaviour, or to divide the day up into a number of observation periods as we did in Example B. Instead of ticks, we shall write in how long the behaviour lasted: '1 minute', '35 minutes', '20 seconds' and so on. If we record every occurrence, our record sheet might look like this:

Example C

Monday	Jimmy rocking					
Time started	How long did behaviour last?	Trigger	Why stopped	People	Place	Other comments
9.05 a.m	8 minutes	waiting for breakfast	Got it	Mother	Kitchen	bored ?
11.15	15 minutes	couldn't get toy	distracted	nobody	living room	seemed resigned
1.20	2 minutes	finished 1st course	got pudding	Mother, Sister	Kitchen	—
4.45	36 minutes	TV on	TV off	Sister	living room	not looking at TV
7.05	about 50 minutes	In cot	went to sleep	nobody	bedroom	banged head too
Total in mins:	111 minutes					

These examples are only to give guidelines. For any particular child, we need to decide the particular questions we want our records to answer, and then use the simplest chart we can to help us to gather the information.

(4) WHAT DO I DO WITH THIS INFORMATION ONCE I'VE GOT IT?

The short answer is – analyse it. This is often easier said than done, however, and we may soon be in danger of being swamped by record-sheets if we don't find some way of pulling our information together.

The easiest way to look back at information we have gathered over a number of weeks is to put it all on to a 'summary chart'. For instance, looking back at Example B (Caroline's tantrums), at the end of each day we shall have a total for every hour of the day and also a 'grand total' for the whole day.

At the end of the week, then, we add up all the totals under '6 a.m.' (for seven different days); then those under '7 a.m.', and so on through the hours; and we also add together the day's totals for the seven days. Then we

can transfer the totals for each week on to a summary chart for several
weeks, which might look something like this:

Example D   Caroline's summary chart

	a.m. 6	7	8	9	10	11	p.m. 12	1	2	3	4	5	6	7	8	9	10	11	Total
Week 1	O	1	6	18	3	2	35	32	2	4	1	6	6	17	2	O	O	1	136
Week 2	O	O	7	21	2	4	33	36	3	3	O	5	6	15	3	O	1	O	139
(Extra if necessary)																			
Programme starts here																			
Week 3	O	1	8	25	3	9	38	37	2	5	2	7	7	19	4	1	O	O	168
Week 4	O	O	4	10	1	2	15	16	1	2	O	3	4	10	2	O	O	O	70
Week 5	O	O	2	4	O	2	7	7	1	3	O	2	3	6	1	O	O	O	38
Week 6	O	O	1	2	O	1	5	4	O	1	O	1	1	3	O	O	O	O	19
Week 7		Stopped Keeping records																	
Week 8																			

Caption: *Frequency of Caroline's tantrums in different hours of day*

If we had an idea that a particular *time of week* was a bad time for
Caroline, we might make an extra chart showing *which days* were important
instead of *which hours*.

Having a simple summary chart like this will save us having to look at a
number of different sheets of paper when we want an idea of the frequency
of the behaviour over time, as well as telling us whether there are any particular days or particular hours within the day which are specially difficult for
our child. If we know which situations seem to encourage this behaviour
(whether we're talking about good or bad behaviour), we shall be better at
working out what to do. For instance, it looks as if mealtimes and bedtime
might be frustrating times for Caroline.

In the same way, we could also draw up summary charts for 'how long'
records, either totting up the total time recorded, or the average time each
day, each week, and at particular times of day.

Notice one thing about Caroline's summary chart: in the first week after
the programme started, her behaviour got worse, not better. This is because
it takes a little while for the child to understand what it's all about. She
knows things have changed, but she hasn't yet got the message clear. She's
used to getting a big reaction when she tantrums; now it's not happening, so
the first thing she tries is to do the same thing but a bit more of it. This is a bit
like the way English people in France, when nobody understands them, may

say the same words but a lot louder! Looking at the second week in the prog-ramme, things are now making much more sense to Caroline, and she does not need to have tantrums so often – they're no longer worth the effort, and she's beginning to find that other, nicer, things happen in the time she used to spend on tantrums.

Also notice that Caroline's parents were happy to 'count as success' a week in which Caroline had less than three tantrums a day: they did not expect her to give up tantrums altogether. They weren't looking for an angel, just for a little girl who could express herself in more useful ways, and who would not feel frustrated so much of the time. Strictly speaking, they should have gone on keeping records for a week or two longer, to make sure the new pattern was firmly established; but they were so pleased with Caroline (and with themselves) that they decided to trust to luck, knowing they could go back to record-keeping if things got worse again.

People often feel put off by the idea of keeping records – we felt that way too! When you get used to it, you'll find it's easier than it looks – and it does work in getting our ideas clear, and therefore in helping us to plan the best possible programme and carry it out. We've tried to keep it simple here. If you want to look at more complicated ways of doing it, you will find other ways of analysing (graphs, histograms and so on) in many of the books recommended for further reading in Appendix 2.

5 Reward and punishment

REWARD

A 'reward' is *anything* that makes behaviour worthwhile for a child. Being rewarded makes it likely that the behaviour will happen again. Roughly speaking, we can look at it like this:

Good behaviour + reward = more good behaviour
Good behaviour + no reward = less good behaviour
Bad behaviour + reward = more bad behaviour
Bad behaviour + no reward = less bad behaviour

A reward which makes behaviour worthwhile is *not necessarily a present.* In fact, far more often in everyday life it is a *response* from someone else. For instance, if we say 'Good morning' to the man next door and he smiles back, we find this *rewarding.* If he consistently ignored our greeting, we should probably give up saying 'Good morning' to him. In other words, we should show less 'greeting behaviour', because we have found it is not worthwhile in this situation. Children behave the same way; they are more likely to approach a neighbour who usually smiles at them than one who ignores or scowls at them.

However, we must remember that a 'reward' does not have to be something that's obviously nice. For instance, most children like attention, and find it rewarding. But sometimes a child may discover that when he is quiet and good, his mother just takes the opportunity to get on with her work and ignores him. (You may remember that this sort of situation came up on page 16.) On the other hand, when he empties the cutlery drawer or pulls down the tablecloth, his mother comes running. The fact that she shouts and maybe smacks him may not be exactly nice, and she certainly doesn't intend it to be; but from the child's point of view, this kind of attention may be more rewarding than no attention at all. So he may go on with this 'attention-seeking behaviour', even though the attention he gets is not obviously pleasant.

41

To change this state of affairs, his mother needs to find a way of giving him a more rewarding kind of attention for his *good* behaviour.

Of course there are some activities which are their own reward – which are pleasant in themselves. For example, activities that most children find rewarding are dabbling in warm water, swinging, swallowing a pleasant drink. In these cases, we do not need to use *extra* rewards; but we may need to organise things so that the rewarding nature of the activity comes over loud and clear.

For instance, the child may be so frightened by the size and slipperiness of the bath that he never gets around to enjoying the feel of the water; or he may sit bored in his swing seat because he can't co-ordinate his movements well enough to get it going, and has nothing nearby to kick off from; or he may so often have choked on a drink that he is now afraid of the cup. These children may at first find it more rewarding to refuse these experiences (because it gets them out of a frightening or boring situation). If we are pretty sure that the experience should be pleasant in itself, then it's our job to think about what is putting the child off, and make sure he gets the chance to attend to and enjoy that pleasure.

We also have to remember that simply being able to do something for yourself, or being good at something, is rewarding even if it's a very small thing. But the child may not always know when he *has* succeeded at something. That means that we have to 'mark' his success: praise him generously, clap, smile at him, shout hooray – whatever comes naturally. 'Nothing succeeds like success' – that is, we all like to *feel* successful, and it spurs us on to try still harder. In time, the child will recognise his own success and will be rewarded by that – then he will no longer need our rewards.

Choosing and using rewards

When we are deciding what rewards to use as part of our teaching plan, parents or foster-parents once again are likely to know better than anyone else what is rewarding to their child – with different children it may be a tiny scrap of chocolate, an affectionate hug or a few words of praise. Some children love a flash of coloured light or a musical sound. The further advanced a child is in his development, the more choice we will have as to possible rewards.

Our message to the child will be clearer if the reward is something a bit *special*. For example, if a child is regularly given crisps all through the day, then he will hardly notice if we give him a crisp as part of our teaching plan. We will either have to restrict crisps to the teaching programme, or maybe decide on something else which we could save for the particular purpose of our teaching. (Actually this is much less true of affectionate attention; children don't seem to get sick of affection the way they get sick of crisps!)

5 Reward and punishment

There are two important rules to remember about giving rewards. Firstly, we must avoid 'bribery'. This is an easy trap to fall into if we are using special rewards. Sometimes we may find it hard to wait for the child to produce the behaviour we want to reward, so we start to coax him into doing it, perhaps by holding out the reward. At this point he is likely to become so interested in grabbing the reward that he forgets about what he needs to do to earn it. We have in fact *distracted* him from the message, instead of making the message clearer, and the result is a shambles. It would be much more helpful to keep the reward out of sight until the moment the behaviour we want occurs.

This brings us to our second important rule. The reward must be given *immediately after* the child does what we want him to do. This is so that it is absolutely clear to the child that *this* is the behaviour we approve of. Sometimes we shall have to be very quick indeed to get this right. For instance, we may want to reward the child just for looking at us when asked, since this is the start of his attending to other things that we need to teach him. But his glance may be very fleeting, and if we are not quick we may find ourselves actually rewarding him for looking away again!

Sometimes he won't actually produce the behaviour we want however long we wait. We may want him to sit down at the table when we ask him to, ready to play with something. But if he is a 'flitting' child, we can ask him till we're blue in the face; there is still no behaviour to reward. To get him going, we may gently bring him to the table and draw him on to the chair; just as his bottom touches the seat, we pop the crisp or scrap of chocolate into his mouth. In this way we have *made the behaviour happen* and then rewarded it *as if* the child had produced it himself. By doing this a number of times, the child begins to link the behaviour both with the request 'sit down' and with the reward. The message becomes clear, and he begins to sit down voluntarily.

> Tammie at five would incessantly wander about the room, never giving her attention to anything for more than two seconds. She only sat down for meals. Her father decided she might enjoy looking at pictures of members of the family in a light-up slide-viewer, while he named them: 'Mummy – Jill – Daddy – Baby – Gran'. However, she never looked into the viewer, only across it as she wandered on. He spent one twenty-minute session pulling Tammie gently on to her chair, saying 'Sit down Tammie' and popping half a raisin in her mouth as she touched the seat. The following evening, when he said 'Sit down Tammie' she stopped wandering and looked at him; after showing her again twice, she sat down herself without being pulled. He continued to reward her for sitting down, and she was now willing to stay sitting for a minute or so.
>
> Now he started feeding her her bedtime cereal as she sat, saying

43

'Look Tammie!' before each spoonful and spooning it in only if she looked at him; if not, he'd put the spoon back in the bowl, wait a moment, then say 'Look Tammie' again. (Don't try this with a main meal; you'll want your child to eat, and you'll find it too hard to put back the spoon when she *doesn't* look!) This took three sessions before Tammie looked more often than not; on the fourth session her father tried it without cereal, just with half-raisins, and it still worked. Putting these two new skills together, he now had a child to whom he could say 'Sit down Tammie – Look!' and she would, mostly, do both. At this point, as she looked at him, he put the bright slide-viewer between his face and hers – and Tammie looked for the first time *into* the viewer and saw what was there, to her great delight. After that, only occasional raisins were needed – she had learned that sitting and looking produced interesting happenings that were worthwhile in themselves.

It is often a good idea to teach the child to respond to some word like 'Look!' which means 'Give me your attention, because something interesting is about to happen'. Once your child understands this fully, it can be the 'getting-down-to-it' signal for many different activities, and save us wasting time frantically waving toys at him when he's got his mind on other things.

We will need to use our common sense about rewards. Once we have decided on our aim, we must make sure that the reward doesn't get in the way of what we want the child to do. For example, if we're trying to get a child to produce a word or sound, stuffing chocolate in his mouth as a reward will make it very difficult for him to produce the next sound! We need to look for a reward that leaves his mouth free. Also, we are not trying to fatten up our children, nor to ruin their teeth if we can help it. In fact it is worth experimenting with a raisin, a morsel of apple or even a single grain of coffee-sugar. Something that *isn't* food is still better, so long as the child finds it rewarding. Rewards don't have to be 'big'. Stroking the hair, saying 'Clever boy!', clapping one's hands or tinkling a musical box may all work for individual children; a quarter-Smartie or half a crisp work just as well as ten – in fact much better, because ten Smarties are quite a distraction!

Chains of reward

In examples like *sitting down* or *looking*, we are concerned with important understandings which the child must get right before he can benefit from further teaching. When we come to teach complex skills, we've already seen that we break these down into a number of steps so that the child learns to manage a *string* of *simple acts*, rather than one very complicated activity. Here we have some choice as to whether we reward for one act at a time, or for two or more acts done in the right order.

44

5   Reward and punishment

Let's take as an example the skill of putting on trousers. To teach this, we first work out the acts or steps that go to make up this complex task. We might decide on a list like this:

(1)   Pick up trousers.
(2)   Hold them the right way round.
(3)   Put one leg in, still holding the trousers.
(4)   Put the other leg in, still holding on.
(5)   Pull trousers up.
(6)   Fasten top.
(7)   Zip up.

For some children, it would be enough just to guide them through the individual steps, gently prompting them where necessary. When we sit by a child encouraging and praising him at each stage, we are in a way using step-by-step rewards. However, at some point the child has to discover the importance of completing the *whole* sequence. He will understand this more easily if we reward increasingly large 'chains' of acts – first one act, then two together, then three, and so on.

For most people, the more natural way to approach this would be by *forward chaining* – that is, we let the child get as far as he can, praise him (or reward him in some other way) for as much as he's done, and then finish the job ourselves. In other words, we begin by rewarding the child when he just picks up his trousers; then we reward him when he picks up the trousers and holds them the right way round; then he has to complete these steps *and* get one leg in, and so on – at each stage he has to get a little bit further forward to get the reward.

The trouble with the forward chaining approach is that in one way it has a built-in sense of failure for the child: every time, we seem to have to finish the job for him. And *failure is not rewarding.*

A better way to leave the child with a sense of achievement is to use *backward chaining*. First we guide the child through all the steps, and reward him *at the end* so that he can see what the goal of the whole task is. Next, we help him through all the stages *except the last*, and we leave him to do the final zip-up. Thus he is rewarded both by us, and by seeing that he has *completed* the task, not just got a little way into it. Once he is zipping-up confidently, we stop helping him at the stage before; so that now he has to fasten the top *and* zip up for the reward. When he's sure of that, we help him as far as getting both legs in, but leave the trousers round his ankles for him to pull up, fasten and zip. And so on. If he needs it, we can give tiny rewards and praise for every step, and a big reward at the end: but we are trying to fade out the step-by-step rewards, because the whole point is that the child should learn to manage the *chain* of acts that is involved in a complex skill. The beauty of backward chaining is that, right from the earliest stage of teaching the skill, we can say to the child 'Terrific, you've finished putting your trousers on yourself!', instead of just 'You've made a good start'. *The child's pride in his own achievement is something we must always work towards.*

PUNISHMENT – OR NON-REWARD?

If we are trying to get rid of a particular kind of behaviour, we shall hope through our observations to discover what is in the situation for the child to find rewarding – that is, the answer to the question 'Why does he go on doing it?' Sometimes, as we have seen, our observations show us that we ourselves are rewarding the child by our own reactions – we're ignoring him when he's being good and then giving him lots of dramatic attention when he throws his food or spits at the baby.

On the whole, the best way of making 'bad' behaviour seem boring and not worthwhile to the child is deliberately to carry out a policy of *non*-reward *while making sure that we do reward 'good' behaviour*. Really this means that we should make sure that *everything worthwhile stops* in response to disruptive behaviour, instead of allowing the more usual situation that everything worthwhile starts. To give a brief example: usually people start giving attention when a child screams in a tantrum; instead, we should react as soon as he *stops* screaming to take a breath. In the same kind of way, if we are feeding a child food that he likes, and he throws it, we would do best to remove both the food and ourselves for three minutes, and so make life as boring as we can for him, rather than making an interesting fuss.

Removing food might look like a punishment; however, our emphasis should be on *reducing the interest in the situation*, rather than creating an unpleasant situation. With this emphasis, we are more likely to remember to provide the *contrasting pleasant experiences* which make the child understand that more co-operative behaviour is worth his while. Sometimes we may remove the child himself from the situation (sometimes called giving the child 'time out'); here again, the message we must try to get over to him is that he can't join in with ordinary interesting family life if he disrupts it, but that we welcome him into it the moment he shows some intention to co-operate.

The trouble with real punishment is that is usually gives the child a very confused message. We've already seen how it can come over to the child as attention, and therefore as reward. It is equally confusing when a smack is used. When a mother smacks, although the smack itself may be short and sharp, the emotions surrounding it are shown over several minutes by the mother's angry words, the expression on her face and often by other 'body language' as well. The problem is that, in those few minutes, the child may well have produced some *good* behaviour, which is now being punished along with the rest. *It is almost impossible for a parent to change in the twinkling of an eye from punishing to rewarding; it is much easier to switch from*

46

non-rewarding to rewarding. For this reason alone, we will do a better job in getting our message clear to the child if we try to steer clear of any kind of emphasis on punishment.

We're not saying that it is a disaster if you lose your temper and smack your child. Most of us have done this at some time. We *are* saying that this is usually to do with emotions and being at one's wits' end, not something that we should deliberately build into a teaching programme.

It is true that some behavioural programmes have tried to use punishment divorced from emotion, and have even gone beyond smacking to such horrific punishments as electric shocks. It seems to us that it is impossible to use such methods while still being interested in human communication. Since it is our whole intention to bring the child into more sensitive communication with his family and keep him there, we would not want to take one step along that route.

As we pointed out in Chapter 2, in some ways the behavioural approach is an unnatural form of communication; 'rewarding' with crisps or praise is a deliberate attempt to set up a more organised or structured situation than is normal or natural, to make things as clear as possible for a child who is easily confused.

Ideally we are hoping to make the child's whole life more rewarding for him, so that he will not need special rewards for these small bits of behaviour. For instance, as time goes on he will find that when he sits down at the table and looks at his mother, things get more exciting in all sorts of ways, because she talks to him and plays with him in this situation. The point is that the handicapped child often doesn't do this naturally: he cannot know that life *is* exciting until he has learned to attend properly, and this is why we have to work out deliberate ways of teaching him these things.

So what now?

SOME QUESTIONS TO ANSWER

Is the *priority for action* which I have chosen
(a)   learning a new skill, or
(b)   reducing or increasing a behaviour which my child already has?
If the priority is 'a new skill', think about the first set of questions below. If it's 'reducing or increasing a behaviour', move on to the second set of questions.

LEARNING A NEW SKILL

• Will I need to break the task down into little steps? What are the steps? Are they small enough and easy enough? (Write them down – it's easier than remembering!)
• What can I do if my child can't manage the first (or last) step, even if I have broken down the skill? (Maybe the step is too big? Maybe he needs me to lead him through it?)
• How am I going to make the behaviour attractive to my child?
• What shall I count as success? In other words, what am I going to reward?
• What am I going to use as a reward? Why this? What are the drawbacks of this reward, or the difficulties in giving it (does it interfere with the next step, for instance)? Is there any other reward which might be easier, smaller or more convenient?
• Is anything likely to get in the way of the message being quite clear?
• Knowing myself, and the relationship I have with my child, what are the kinds of mistake *I* am likely to make in making my messages clear?
• Where and when am I going to carry out my teaching programme? Why there? Why then? How often?
• Is this something I really feel that I can handle, or does anything about it worry me?
• Who else needs to be involved in the teaching programme? Do they understand and agree with the rewards I'm using?
• Whom could I get to watch me, to check that the rewarding is happening as I intend it to?
• How am I going to keep notes of my programme? (Make it simple!)

REDUCING OR INCREASING BEHAVIOUR

• How have I tried to reduce or increase this behaviour before? How well did it work? Is there anything I can learn from this (for instance, what made my message confusing for the child)?

48

5 Reward and punishment

- What *exactly* is the message I am trying to give my child? (Write it down – it will help you to get it clear.) What am I trying to encourage him to do?
- What is making my child's present behaviour worthwhile?
- What rewards am I going to use for behaviour I'm trying to increase? How am I going to 'non-reward' behaviour that I'm trying to reduce? Why have I chosen this? Are these the easiest and most convenient rewards and non-rewards I could choose?
- How am I going to make sure I time my rewarding, or non-rewarding, properly (i.e. do it at the right moment)?
- If I'm reducing this behaviour, what alternative activity am I trying to put in its place? Is that attractive enough in itself? How can I make it more attractive to my child?
- What else can I do to make my messages quite clear?
- What do I count as *success*? In other words, what behaviour am I going to reward?
- If I'm trying to reduce behaviour, what exactly counts as the behaviour I'm going to non-reward?
- Where and when am I going to carry out my teaching programme? Why there? At what time of day? Why then? How often? Are there any disadvantages?
- Knowing myself, and the relationship I've built up with my child, what mistakes might I make in trying to make my messages clear?
- Is the teaching programme something I feel I can handle, or do parts of it worry me?
- Some of the behaviour I'm trying to reduce will probably get worse at first. Just what is my child likely to do when I start non-rewarding? How will I (and other members of the family) cope with that?
- Who else needs to be involved in the teaching programme? Do they understand and agree with the rewards or non-rewards which I have chosen?
- Whom can I get to watch me, to check that the rewarding, or non-rewarding, is happening the way I intend it to?
- How am I going to keep notes of what happens, so as to be sure what's going on?

SMACKING

Here's an example of how easy it is to give the child a confusing message when you smack.

> Martin was a partially deaf autistic boy who spent a great deal of his time screaming. This made life very stressful for his mother, and it was also preventing Martin from learning to talk: you can't say words when your mouth is full of scream! Martin's mother felt

things were going too slowly, and in desperation she told the psychologist that she'd decided to smack Martin every time he screamed. The psychologist agreed that she should try it if she wanted to, but warned her that it was a difficult method to use clearly, and that she might also find that Martin actually enjoyed the attention of a smack.

At that moment Martin screamed, and Martin's mother quickly smacked him, saying angrily '*Don't* do that!' Martin was taken by surprise, and said 'Oooooooh . . .!' Now this utterance was a very good sound, more like a real conversational word than any he had made for some days, and just what we were trying to encourage. However, Martin's mother was still feeling the anger that had belonged to the smack, and she was still frowning and glaring at him – so the good 'Ooooh . . .' sound got punished along with the screaming. She was naturally very surprised when the psychologist hugged Martin and said 'Good boy, Martin, lovely sound!' As we said in this chapter, it's almost impossible to switch in a second from punishing to rewarding; this is why we try to use 'non-reward' rather than real punishments.

NOTES FOR ACTION

Some of these might be helpful:
(1)   Keep a pencil and paper around to jot down useful ideas that occur to you while you're doing other things.
(2)   It may be useful to spend a few days just observing your child. Try answering these questions.
  ● *What kinds of things give him pleasure?*
  Social rewards
      smiling?
      hug, kiss?
      touching?
      clap?
      'good boy', 'fantastic' etc.?
  Objects
      food, drink (what kind?) . . . .?
      something to hold . . . .?
      other . . . .?
  Sensations
      music?
      other sound . . . .?
      light flashing?
      stroking, patting . . . .?
      water, fur etc.?

5 *Reward and punishment*

- *What does he* not *like?* (Avoid these for the moment – later we might teach him to like them if it seems important.)
feeling unsteady?
being touched?
loud noises?
high noises?
feel of certain things?
taste of certain things?
etc. . . . .

(3)   Perhaps other people know things about him that you don't. What answers would other people in the family (or his teacher, or babysitter) give to the questions in (2)? Ask them – you need all the help you can get.

(4)   If your child does have a lot to do with other people, get them to help. Explain what you're doing, so that they can back you up by making sure the child gets the same messages from them.

(5)   Once we've got started on a teaching programme, it's often useful to ask someone else to watch us rewarding our child – just to check whether what *we* think is going on is what's actually happening. It's easy to miss something important when you're part of the action. An observer may not necessarily be right, but another point of view is always helpful.

6 Examples of a behavioural approach: dressing, toileting, feeding

In the last four chapters we have looked at how we might go about helping our child to change his behaviour, either by teaching new skills, or by decreasing behaviour that gets in the way of his development.

This chapter will look at how we might use a behavioural approach in three everyday activities to help our child become more independent. For most children, independence is a pleasure and reward in itself; and if he can do things for himself, this also gives us more time and energy for other activities with him.

Because handicapped children are bound to be dependent on their parents in more ways and for a longer time than ordinary children, it is all too easy to find that we are doing more for them than is in their interests. Even with ordinary children, parents can get into the habit of doing too much for the child – often it's easier and quicker to do it yourself than to be patient while the child struggles with it. Handicapped children are likely to encourage their parents to be too protective, both because they *are* more helpless, and because they are often fond of routine and quite content to sit back forever and let things be done for them. Some psychologists think that children can *learn to be helpless* in the same way that they learn skills; in other words, if we do too much for our child, the message we are giving him is that he is incapable of doing things for himself. We need instead to give him the confidence to try, the motivation to persist and the skill to succeed. We are helping him to think of himself as a CAN person, not a CAN'T and WON'T person.

As before, we need first to write down what our child can do now; secondly, to decide what we want him to be able to do; and, thirdly, to work out the steps to reach that goal. Then we can set out on our programme. We must also be clear about what behaviour we are going to reward, and what reward we are going to use; and we must be consistent in our rewarding and careful not to reward behaviour that gets in the way of his success.

52

Another thing we can do from the start is to look carefully at the task to see whether we can make it any easier for him. Some children may have physical handicaps, and what they can do is limited by that. Sometimes, though, we may be able to let a child achieve at least some success, in dressing for example, by using easy-fitting clothes, perhaps replacing zips or buttons with velcro, using elastic instead of fastenings or belts, having clothes that do up in front, and so on. Later, we will probably want to move on to the complicated yet normal fasteners like zips, buttons, shoe laces, press-studs, buckles and hooks; but to begin with, while we are building up the child's confidence, it's a good idea to stick to clothes which are easy to put on and take off. Similarly, there are special mugs, plates, spoons and so on which are designed to make feeding skills easier to start with.

DRESSING

Let's think about a particular example. Suppose we have checked how far our child can already help in dressing himself, and which fasteners he can handle at all, and we decide that he is probably physically capable of putting on his jumper. The reward for each successful step, we may have decided, will be clapping our hands and saying 'good boy' enthusiastically, and for completing the final step he will get a crisp or raisin. (We try not to use food or a hug *during* the sequences because it is too distracting and interferes with the smooth flow.) If he refuses to co-operate, for the moment we will firmly ignore him, apart from returning the jumper to his hands and saying 'Go on, put your jumper on'.

We will need to break down the task of putting on a jumper into a number of small steps. The first might be to pick it up in such a way that there is a 'way in'; the second to get his head inside; the third to pull the jumper down round his neck; the fourth to put one arm into its sleeve; the fifth to get the other arm in; and the last step to pull the jumper down over the waist. Depending on the individual child, we may need to break things down into still smaller steps or to alter things slightly; for instance, if our child has problems with balance, we may want to do some of the steps sitting down.

You may remember from Chapter 5 that this kind of activity is often best taught backwards, when it is known as 'backward chaining'. In other words, to start with we 'do all the work' except the last step – letting our child pull his jumper down at the end – and if he makes an effort to finish the task, we reward him (crisp or raisin) immediately. Once we are sure that he can do the last step for himself, we then should expect him to do the last *two* steps for himself, then the last three, and so on, till he can do all six steps for himself. At first we can praise him and clap for each step (if he seems to need it),

53

giving a crisp for the last one; gradually, we can 'fade out' the step-by-step rewards, and just reward him at the end.

Suppose my child just refuses?

You may be thinking 'It's all very well telling us to "firmly ignore him" if he won't co-operate – we could ignore our child all day and he'd never be any nearer putting his jumper on'. That's perfectly true, and we only try ignoring to see if it will work – if it doesn't (having given it a good chance), we have to have another method up our sleeve.

If the child won't co-operate and is only too happy to be ignored, we're not going to leave it at that. Somehow we've got to help him to know *what it feels like to co-operate and be successful.* If he won't get that experience for himself, we must deliberately make it happen for him.

The way we can do this is to try backward chaining again, but this time to 'prompt': *put the child through the actions* that we expect of him. So for the last step we put our hands around his (standing behind him is probably easiest), curl his fingers firmly round the bottom edge of his jumper and pull it down. Then, quickly, we reward him *as if he had done it himself.* This way we give him a taste of success.

After a number of experiences of this (some children need more than others), he will begin to grip and pull the jumper down for himself, first with your hands only loosely around his, then without your help at all. At this stage you can go back to the previous step, doing everything yourself until putting the second arm in, then helping him through that action and praising him for it; then leaving him to do the final pulling down himself, with the crisp or raisin as a reward. And so on, back through the chain – each time giving him the experience of doing the action for a reward. The point is that it's almost impossible to *explain* to the child that he might actually find it worth while to co-operate, so you have to *show* him. As he begins to see the point, we can fade out our help.

Two things to remember all the way through. Firstly, the child is supposed to enjoy this – and so might we! If we try too intensely or get worked up about it, our child will feel less like playing along; he may even sense our tension, and become really resistant. So make it fun, keep it light – and if it seems to be one of those days when nothing will work, forget it till tomorrow.

Secondly, we shouldn't make too many demands too quickly. It is better – and more likely to be successful – if we regularly expect our child to do just a little, than if we pressure him to get through a number of steps at once. It needs a lot of patience to take things slowly and steadily – parents need rewarding too! Sometimes he *will* make a sudden rapid improvement, as if a 'penny dropped'. Take that as a bonus, but don't expect him to make rapid improvements every day or every week.

TOILETING

Children vary a lot as to when they are ready to begin toilet-training. A child's ability to control his bladder is a mixture of the *physical* (that is, the child must be able to control the right muscles, and must be free from any bladder infections) and the *psychological* (it must seem worthwhile to him). Some toilet-training problems do have physical causes, and you will need to know whether there are any medical reasons which might make toileting difficult. Ask your doctor about this.

Before trying to toilet-train our child we need to know that he is ready. This means making some observations first to see if he shows any pattern of wetting. For three separate two-hour periods in the day, we check every fifteen minutes whether our child is wet or dry, and make a note each time. We do this for a week, by which time we should have seven sets of 27 observations. This may seem a lot, but it's worth doing, rather than trying to train a child who isn't ready. If at the same time we make sure that our child isn't eating and drinking very differently from usual, we should get a fairly clear idea of whether there is any pattern to his bladder or bowel control. For example, he may wet roughly every hour or every hour and a half, or he may have a bowel movement around 10.00 a.m. each day.

If there is no regular pattern at all, it may well be that our child is not ready to begin toilet training yet. But if there is a pattern, we can begin our programme by using what we have learned of his bladder habits. We start by giving him slightly *more* liquid than usual, then just before the time we could normally expect him to wet, we would take him to the potty or toilet (and it might be a good idea to keep the potty in the toilet, so that he learns to associate the two). If the child does use the toilet or potty, we must tell him how pleased we are and reward him immediately. At this stage a small drink is a good reward, as we want lots of opportunities to take him to the toilet with a full bladder. Some parents find a musical box to play a little tune makes a good reward, or a torch which flashes different colours. We can use whatever best suits ourselves and the child.

In general, we must make sure that the toilet or potty is not uncomfortable for him, nor easily overbalanced; we shouldn't leave him sitting by himself; and we should not expect him to sit for long periods – all of these things will be teaching him that potties or toilets are unpleasant. Flushing the toilet without warning might have the same effect, though for many children flushing can be used as a reward. Some children accept the potty more happily if they can hold a familiar toy or object, and we should encourage anything which makes the child feel more comfortable. Simple pants which are easy to take down will also help.

If he does not use the potty, but starts to have an 'accident' later on, we should quickly, and without fuss, take him to the toilet or potty. Even a few drops should be rewarded. Most children will continue to have occasional accidents, and these should be dealt with calmly. Lots of parents find they get upset and worked up over wet pants; but this is the quickest way either to make the child panicky (in which case he'll wet himself *more* often), or to teach him to use wetting himself just to get attention.

FEEDING

Once again, where we start will depend on what our child can do now. During their first year most babies learn a lot about using their tongues to suck and to move the food around their mouths; using their lips to keep food and liquid in their mouths; using jaws and teeth to make the food fit to swallow; and using throat muscles to send it on its way down. What's more, they use these different parts in *co-ordination* – lips and tongue work together, so do tongue and throat muscles. Being able to control jaw, lips, tongue and throat muscles is an important part of being able to speak clearly; learning to eat properly gives a very good basis for our child's later speech development.

If our child has physical difficulty with this kind of control, we shall need individual advice from his physiotherapist. Don't be afraid to ask questions! Some children need to be deliberately taught to bite, chew or swallow, and the physiotherapist will suggest special techniques and ways of helping.

In general, it is worth giving some thought to making mealtimes a pleasure. Like toilet-training, mealtimes can easily become battlegrounds, and parents can find themselves under stress – especially if they are anxious that the child is not eating enough, or if the food they have so lovingly prepared is thrown across the room!

How can we make mealtimes more enjoyable? Well, for a start we could ask ourselves a few questions from the child's point of view.

• *Did we give him time to anticipate the meal with pleasure* or did we just grab him? Some children don't like being suddenly taken from what they are doing and plonked at the table. It's a good idea to talk cheerfully about the fact that it's nearly dinner time as you do the final preparation.

• *Is he sitting comfortably?* Make sure he feels stable and well-supported – that he isn't half-slipping off his seat.

• *Is he surrounded by temptations?* If you put a 'grabber' or 'flinger' where he can reach the salt, pepper, glasses and other people's food, you're asking for trouble. Clear a space round him and introduce these opportunities *very* gradually. If he's inclined to run off, hem him in a little – in a high chair if he's small, or between father and the wall perhaps. Use a light strap-harness for the moment rather than have constant battles and chasings.

• *Is the food attractive?* It's worth taking trouble with colour – drab food is not appetising. Pink milk can be persuasive! Does the food smell nice? If you're feeding the child yourself and he's very slow, use a bowl of hot

56

water to stand the plate on to keep it warm. Give small portions on a large plate to make it look less overwhelming.

• *Is every mouthful a nasty shock?* If you are spoon-feeding, make sure the child has time to get ready for each spoonful. He needs to see it coming; if the child's posture is awkward, or if he tends to turn his face away, you may have to take a new angle of approach so that he can see the spoon as it comes. Otherwise he may feel that every spoonful is an attack on his mouth – and there's no quicker way to put a child off mealtimes.

• *Are we able to give him enough attention?* If you are pulled in all directions by serving up, looking after other children and worrying whether the pudding's burning, it will be difficult to make your child's meal relaxed and enjoyable. Share out the jobs if you can. If you can't, consider whether it would be better to feed your handicapped child separately for a while, at least until mealtimes regularly go smoothly for him.

Finger-feeding

Having made mealtimes as pleasant as we can, how should we go about helping the child to feed himself and to use a spoon? We've put it in that order because most children 'finger-feed' themselves before they get around to using a spoon, and some do need help in learning to finger-feed. It's usually a waste of time trying to get a child to use a spoon himself if he isn't yet finger-feeding freely.

Suppose your child so far has just opened his mouth like a baby bird for someone else to spoon in the food: he needs to understand the basic fact that he might get that food to his mouth himself. Look for food that you know he likes, and at the beginning of the mealtime scatter it on his high-chair tray (or on a small tray in front of him) in bite-sized pieces. Bits of crisp bacon, apple slices, small pineapple chunks, raisins, pieces of biscuit, crisps, twiglets, cheese cubes – all of these are good examples, but choose whatever might tempt your child. If you like, dip a rusk in honey, rosehip syrup or melted chocolate – he'll make a bit of a mess, but it'll teach him to lick and suck for himself.

Give him a little help to get the idea, but *don't* get conned into feeding him every piece, or you'll be no further on. You may have to be a bit hard-hearted if he is used to you feeding him every mouthful. The reason we choose the beginning of the meal is because he'll be hungry then, and more inclined to make an effort. If he is very resistant, though, it might be best to make it a meal you don't mind about, so that *you* don't get too anxious if he just flings the food about. Lots of parents can stay calm while their child wastes his breakfast or tea, but will rush in to feed him his dinner. If you feel like that, choose breakfast or teatime for making him work for his food.

If your child has erratic movements that make it difficult for him to 'aim' at his mouth, special seating or side wedges may help his arm control – again, consult his physiotherapist.

Spoon-feeding

Once a child is used to finger-feeding (which means that he can bring something to his mouth without dropping it), then chances are that he is ready to use a spoon, even though that is a good deal more difficult. We can try to make things easier for him to start with in a number of ways:

• Choose a spoon that is easy to hold (look for one with a slightly chunky handle, maybe from an antique stall – odd ones can be cheaper than new). Make sure the bowl of the spoon fits his mouth comfortably.

• Use a non-tip bowl or plate; some have a rubber ring to prevent slipping, or you can use a rubber mat. Special tableware can be bought; the spoons are angled to make aiming easier, and the plates and bowls have one vertical side, which gives the spoon something to push against. You may find it worth looking at these aids, although obviously it will be more convenient if in the end your child learns to manage ordinary table things.

• If possible, start off by using food that is easy to spoon, so long as your child likes it. Something of the consistency of semolina pudding or mashed potato or thickened soup is ideal, because a little bit will stick to the spoon anyway, even if the child manipulates the spoon clumsily. If your child likes none of these, try flavouring one of them with something he does like (chocolate potato, for instance?) for the sake of building-in success from the very beginning.

Now, as before, let's break down the activity of using a spoon, and work out the steps involved. They are:

(1)   Pick up the spoon.
(2)   Dip and fill it.
(3)   Move it from plate to mouth *without* turning it over and losing the contents.
(4)   Adjust the angle of the spoon to place it between the lips.
(5)   Empty the spoon into the mouth without spilling.
(6)   Take the empty spoon from his mouth.

(If at this point he usually drops the spoon on the floor, we may have to add another step: putting it back on the plate.)

It may again be best to go about teaching this skill 'backwards'. So, to begin with, we would expect our child to grasp the spoon in his hand; but we would curl our own fingers round his to keep it there, and to guide the filling of the spoon, help him to bring it up to his mouth, help him empty it – then let go of his hand at this point and praise him when he takes the spoon from his mouth. When he has mastered this, we would take our hand from his at the moment when the spoon enters his mouth. The next stage would be to help him fill the spoon, but expect him to get it to his mouth and out again . . . and so on.

Obviously it's not appropriate to reward with food as the child is eating already. If you have managed to choose a food he likes his action will be automatically rewarded, and you need only add praise. If you find you do need another reward, try a sip of juice, a few turns of a musical box, stroking his hair or clapping your hands.

What if he throws, spatters or spits the food instead of eating it? If this often happens, you will already have provided good overalls for both yourself and the child, and newspaper on the floor, so that you can stay calm and cool; and you'll have made it difficult for him to reach any food but his own. The moment that he misuses his food, remove the plate, turn your back on him, and count to 30 (nothing magic about the number – vary it to suit yourself). Then turn back to him and start again, CALMLY, where you left off. If he throws again, remove food and turn away again, perhaps for a little longer this time. If it keeps on, remove the food altogether, clean up and DON'T RELENT, but try again in an hour.

It's important not to get upset, and to do what you mean to do without fuss. That way, your child is not confused by your emotions, and is more likely to get the message that it's just not worth his while to throw or spit.

Once again, we must remember that different children learn at different speeds, and each step may take a long time for one particular child. We should try not to push the child so hard that learning is unenjoyable. Let him know how much you appreciate his achievement, but don't let him think you won't love him *unless* he achieves.

Shaping

Sometimes, as we saw in the 'in-between' behaviour on page 22, a child will show the *beginnings* of the kind of behaviour we're looking for, but no more. For instance, he may pick up the spoon, fill it and then just wave it about. This is better than nothing – though it may not seem so as we mop up the gobbets of pudding. We would like to reward him for getting the spoon into his mouth, but this is hardly happening at all. So we may decide to reward him when he waves it nearer than usual, to give him the idea gradually. We might first reward him just for bending his arm when he's holding the spoon; then when he's doing that more often, we might only reward him if he gets the spoon within two inches of his mouth; when that increases, only when the spoon touches his mouth; and finally, only if it gets inside, which was our original idea.

This does take quite a long time, and it can be useful to use a little prompting (helping his hand in the right direction and rewarding him as if he'd done it himself) at the same time.

Shaping can often be a useful method when helping a child to make his screams or squeals into sounds that are more bearable and more communicative: by rewarding first any sound that is *not* a squeal, and then gradually saving our rewards for more and more 'speech-like' noises, we can show the child a better way of getting through to us. Eventually this will also get him ready to imitate real words.

6 Examples of a behavioural approach

In this chapter we have tried to look at a behavioural approach to the every-day activities of dressing, toileting and feeding, all of which can be difficult for a handicapped child. These particular examples may not all be a problem for your child, but perhaps they have shown you how we can apply to a number of different situations what we have learned about looking at behaviour and getting messages across.

The next three chapters take a slightly different approach. You will have noticed that we keep talking about making learning *enjoyable* for children. The two chapters that follow will look at the whole area of play, and its importance in every child's development. Chapter 9 will deal with first steps towards language – in other words, with what a child needs to understand before his language can develop.

So what now?

It is probably time now to take stock of the main points contained in Chapters 2–6. The quiz below is designed for this purpose. Simply choose which of the statements is the best way to complete the sentences.

Answers are given at the end. If you have any trouble with the questions, it is worth checking back to the chapters which contain the information.

1   (Chapter 2) *The idea behind the behavioural approach is that –*
       A. Children need bribing to be good.
       B. Children learn their behaviour from the messages we give them.
       C. Children can't learn until they can talk.

2   (Chapter 2) *We learn particular kinds of behaviour –*
       A. Because we find that particular behaviour worthwhile for us.
       B. Because people tell us to do the right things.
       C. Because otherwise we'll be punished.

3   (Chapter 2) *The main aim of the behavioural approach in this handbook is –*
       A. To control our child's behaviour.
       B. To help our child know right from wrong.
       C. To help us get over to our child that certain behaviours are worthwhile to him.

4   (Chapter 3) *The very first step in planning a programme for our child is –*
       A. To decide what our rewards will be.
       B. To find out what our child can and can't do now.
       C. To ask a psychologist to measure his IQ.

5   (Chapter 3) *If we are trying to stop a particular behaviour, we will need to know –*
       A. Exactly what happens and what might be making it worthwhile for our child.
       B. How to punish our child so that he understands in future.
       C. Where he gets all his energy from.

6   (Chapter 3) *If we are hoping to teach him a new behaviour, we will need firstly –*
       A. To be able to describe accurately the new behaviour and all its steps.

61

6   *Examples of a behavioural approach*

   B. To show our child what we want him to do.
   C. To buy a box of smarties.

7   (Chapter 4) *The two main types of records we can keep are –*
   A. *How far* and *how loud.*
   B. *How stressful* and *how tiring.*
   C. *How long* and *how often.*

8   (Chapter 4) *If the behaviour we're working on is frequent, the best way to record it is –*
   A. Every time it happens.
   B. For a certain length of time at different periods throughout the day.
   C. Whenever we have time.

9   (Chapter 4) *If the behaviour is infrequent, the best way to record it is –*
   A. Every time, to see if there is a pattern.
   B. At certain periods throughout the day, to see if it stops.
   C. At mealtimes.

10   (Chapter 4) *We need first to record our child's present behaviour for a week or two –*
   A. Because we want him to know we're recording.
   B. Because it helps us know exactly what it is that we are trying to change, and lets us judge how much progress is made later.
   C. Because it makes us feel as though we're doing something useful right from the start.

11   (Chapter 4) *During the first week of a programme to change 'bad' behaviour, we're likely to find that –*
   A. Our child will try very hard to please us, because he knows we might be disappointed in him.
   B. Our child's behaviour will be really good because he's looking forward to rewards all the time.
   C. Our child's bad behaviour will increase, because he's confused by the change.

12   (Chapter 5) *Rewards are –*
   A. Anything that's nice.
   B. Anything which makes behaviour worthwhile for a person.
   C. Any kind of present.

13   (Chapter 5) *In our programmes we should choose as rewards –*

   A. Something nice for our child to eat.
   B. Hugs and kisses.
   C. Anything special and convenient to give which we think might increase the behaviour we want.

14   (Chapter 5) *The reward should be given –*
   A. Immediately after he shows (or partly shows) the behaviour we are trying to get.
   B. Whatever our child does, to give him encouragement.
   C. Beforehand, to get our child to do what we want.

15   (Chapter 5) *We should show our child his reward –*
   A. Right at the beginning, to get him interested in the programme.
   B. Only after he has achieved at least some of the behaviour we're looking for.
   C. Every so often, to remind him what he's supposed to be aiming for.

16   (Chapter 5) *If we 'non-reward' behaviour, we are trying –*
   A. To punish our child.
   B. To pretend we don't care about it.
   C. To stop the behaviour being worthwhile.

17   (Chapter 5) *When 'non-rewarding' behaviour, it is very important –*
   A. To reward any good behaviour he shows.
   B. To let our child know we are not pleased with him.
   C. To keep a straight face.

18   (Chapter 5) *The main problem with punishing our child is –*
   A. It makes us feel guilty.
   B. We might be giving a mixed-up message.
   C. It never works.

19   (Chapter 5) *If we, or anyone involved with our child, are inconsistent in rewarding or 'non-rewarding' him during the programme –*
   A. We'll need to start again from scratch.
   B. It doesn't matter because it teaches him we're human.
   C. He is learning that the behaviour is still worthwhile.

20   (Chapter 5) *We would hope to reward our child less and less often as time goes on –*
   A. Because he will get bored with rewards.

6 Examples of a behavioural approach

B. Because he's got to learn that he can't expect rewards all the time.

C. Because we're trying to make the behaviour rewarding in itself.

21   (Chapter 6) *When we are trying to chain behaviour –*

A. We must not be satisfied unless the child completes the whole chain.

B. We must make sure the steps are small enough for the child to keep adding a step.

C. We must explain to the child how many steps will get a reward.

22   (Chapter 6) *In backward chaining, we reward our child –*

A. When he starts off an action like putting on his trousers.

B. When he completes an action like putting on his trousers.

C. When he helps a bit from time to time.

23   (Chapter 6) *If our child just won't do the action we are trying to teach him –*

A. We should design a new programme.

B. We should try punishing him for not doing it.

C. We should guide him, and then reward him as though he had done it himself.

24   (Chapter 6) *The behavioural approach is –*

A. Mainly useful for getting rid of unacceptable behaviour in handicapped children.

B. Mainly useful for calming down disturbed or hyperactive children.

C. Mainly useful because it can help a child to develop his skills as well as reduce behaviour that gets in the way of development.

ANSWERS

1B, 2A, 3C, 4B, 5A, 6A, 7C, 8B, 9A, 10B, 11C, 12B, 13C, 14A, 15B, 16C, 17A, 18B, 19C, 20C, 21B, 22B, 23C, 24C.

7 Play: what are the problems?

In this chapter we shall look at what play is and how useful it is to children; and we shall see how handicapped children can find it difficult to play. In the next chapter we will look at how we might plan play for handicapped children in order to get round some of the difficulties or at least reduce them.

Let us first try to define what we mean by the word 'play'. Perhaps it is easiest to think of play as the *way* a child does something, rather than *what* he does. Play doesn't have to be something a child does with toys, or what we can recognise as a game: it is the child's *feeling* about it that matters. Play is fun; play is pleasurable; play is *playful*. Being forced to 'play' by an adult is not play; being invited to, and choosing whether or not to accept, is. In other words, play is voluntary. Successful play can be as rewarding for parents as it is for children.

Adults tend to think of play as recreation – what they do in their spare time. But it would be wrong to assume that a child's play doesn't much matter, simply because it is not part of what adults think of as the real world or because it doesn't look like our idea of education. In fact, for all children, play, and the ability and opportunity to play, are a very important part of development. Through play, a child can learn things which will develop not only his bodily co-ordination, but also his thoughts and his language. He will see what happens if you bang, twist, prod or pull objects, and what happens if two particular objects hit each other (they might make different sounds for instance, or different movements). He may use a play situation to learn new words and work out ways of putting them together, at first from his parents, but later from his own playmates; or to try out behaviour or ways of reacting to other people which he has heard or seen others use. This is using play to learn about and experiment with *social* behaviour.

In a 'normal' pattern of progress, the kinds of play a child can cope with are obviously decided by what stage of development he has reached. This means both what he is capable of in the way of managing his limbs and balance, using hands and fingers, putting his thoughts into words, and so on –

65

and also how much he can do *for himself* without help. Early in life, a baby is very dependent on a parent to provide opportunities for play, and things to play with. 'Play' at this stage might mean looking at interesting things like a mobile or floating bubbles, and watching how they move and change; lap play, like peep-bo or 'this little piggy'; grasping or shaking simple objects, and so on. Parents also provide some variety in playthings or play situations; and by joining in the baby's play, they suggest to him new ways of playing with the same object.

Gradually, as the normal child becomes more mobile and more skilled, the need for a parent to *set up* situations disappears – though obviously the child still needs opportunities to be provided, and still appreciates his parents' interest and involvement in his play. Later still, of course, as the child becomes socially more independent, parents' involvement tends to be largely replaced by playmates. The children begin to work out between themselves how they will play, and games involving rules begin to be important to them. Their 'pretend' play may have quite a complicated story to it. At the same time, many children continue to have their own private games of 'pretend' as well. For most children it is *emotionally* very satisfying to be able to create play situations for themselves, with or without other children – independence is a pleasure for the growing child.

Play is not just a way of passing the time pleasantly. Real learning – in manual skills, bodily co-ordination, language, social behaviour or intellectual understanding – takes place when the child explores and experiments with people and things around him: in other words, throughout his play. What he learns in his play in turn affects the way he copes with the 'real' world and 'real' life. A growing child uses his play to make sense of the world around him.

PLAY AND HANDICAP

For a handicapped child, the implications of this last statement are enormous. If a child's opportunities for play are limited because he is restricted by a particular handicap, this is likely to mean that his opportunities for development in many areas – physical, social, intellectual and emotional – are at once affected as a result.

One child may find it physically difficult to hold and finger objects or to move his limbs in the way he wants to; or even to get himself across the carpet. Another may have visual problems: this in itself makes him less mobile, because he's scared to move around in space he can't see properly. Poor vision also means that he cannot look around and see where a toy is in order to get it, nor can he see the details of it once it is in his hands. Some children are withdrawn and inward-turning, perhaps because they have such difficulty in making sense of what they see and hear that they are overwhelmed by a fear of the unknown. Others are hyperactive or 'flitting'; they seem driven on by their own physical energy, and they are unable to stop, look and concentrate on one activity for more than a few seconds.

Handicapped children will be far more dependent on having an adult playmate and 'provider', and for much longer, than ordinary children. Without the attention, understanding, imagination and patience of an adult, most of the handicapped child's opportunities to learn and develop through play would not exist. However, in our enthusiasm to help the child to learn we must not forget the *voluntary* and *exploratory* nature of play. We are not trying to drill the child into learning; we need to set up opportunities which will allow him to find out that play *is* fun, and worth the extra effort that it takes for him. We *invite* the child to play, and we try to make it possible for him to accept our invitation.

In all this, our aim when we play with him is not only to help the child to want to learn new skills, but also to give him the feeling that he has some mastery and control over the things around him. This is an important part of learning to be a *person*, and not just a helpless baby.

Much of what we have discussed in previous chapters is clearly going to be useful here, both in assessing each child's difficulties and in meeting his needs. Your local toy library will also help you, not only by lending toys suitable for your child, but also with suggestions and ideas on how you can introduce particular toys most successfully, what you might expect and encourage your child to do, and what might be going wrong where things don't seem to be working out. We must remember, though, that a toy, however attractive, is *not* something that we can give the child so as not to have to play with him ourselves. At its best, the toy is one more means through which we can learn to communicate better with our child. In the process, he is likely to learn something about his world, and about us too.

Perhaps you are now doubting whether this chapter is useful in your own child's case. Parents of handicapped children often feel that their child simply *does not* play. It is true that young handicapped children often appear to have no desire to play or explore. It may help us to try to see this from the child's point of view. If we look at the child's behaviour as his attempt to make sense of his world – remembering that he may feel he has no control over it – we can then try to *think ourselves into* his handicap. Do the noises that his toys make help him to understand them better – or do they frighten and confuse him? Are his toys full of unpleasant surprises? (Most children like surprises that they are half-expecting!) Would *you* be bored with this toy if you had his handicap – or perhaps find it too complicated to see the point of? Has he given up in despair because he can't hold on long enough, or concentrate long enough, to get to the toy's most exciting moment – its 'payoff'?

Thinking ourselves into the child's skin like this can often make us realise why he is not finding it pleasant to play. We are then halfway to working out ways of making play both possible and rewarding for him.

The next chapter will give some examples of planning play for children with various kinds of special problems. It is not intended as a set of recipes, but to illustrate how we can think about an individual difficulty and work towards solving it. Even if your own child does not have the particular problems given in these examples, it is how we *approach* the child's needs that matters. The goals are the same for every child: to plan his play in such a way that (1) he is enabled to enjoy the activity; (2) he learns to attend and co-operate long enough to carry through to the 'pay-off' (and therefore experiences success); (3) his play helps him to communicate with his parents; and (4) he develops a little further his sense of mastering what may for him be a very confusing world.

So what now?

'A growing child uses his play to make sense of the world around him.'

That's probably the most important sentence in Chapter 7, because it's our job to make play work in the same way for our handicapped child as it does for other children. Play may not come naturally to him, but we can still find ways of making it happen and making it useful. If that helps him to make sense of the world around him, obviously it's worth a lot of effort from us.

When you come to think about it, the word 'sense' can be used in two rather different ways. We've used it here as 'meaning': *making sense* of things is the same as *getting meaning* from them. But we also talk about 'the five senses' – hearing, seeing, smelling, tasting and touching.

We use these five senses to get bits of information which we can then put together (using our brain) in order to make sense or get meaning. The bits of information on their own are not much use until we can make sense of them by working on them in this way. All the same, the more practice we get in *attending to* what our senses tell us, the better we shall be able to put our bits of information together in order to get at their meaning.

We can help a handicapped child to attend to what his senses are telling him by the way we play with him, and we can also help him to learn about meaning by making sure that there *is* a meaning for him, and helping him to find it. If our child has a damaged or lost sense – if for instance he is partly or wholly blind, or deaf, or both – he will all the more need our help to get the best information he can from the senses that are left to him, and make it meaningful.

In fact, we might do better to use different words to describe the five senses. Words like 'see' and 'hear' are a little bit passive, and in fact remind us that most of us can't help seeing and hearing the sights and sounds that pour into our eyes and ears. But if we are going to concentrate on meaning, we should be trying to make our child an *actively* sensing person. That means that we must help him not just to hear, but to *listen*; not just see, but *look*; not smell, but *sniff to get the smell*; not passively taste, but *actively savour*; not merely touch, but *feel and explore*.

Let's think now about how we can make him aware of all these possibilities.

HELPING A CHILD TO LISTEN

Firstly, if you normally have 'wallpaper music' on just for company (or to soothe your child), remember that this damps down other sounds and teaches him *not* to listen. Ration yourself!

69

We want him to realise

- that there are *lots of different sounds*. Listen for different sounds yourself, and show him you're listening in an exaggerated 'acting' way – finger on lips, eyes open wide – to try to get him to listen too. Make sounds happen yourself, close to his ear if they're tiny sounds – rustling paper or cellophane, ticking watch, ballpoint click – and get him to make the sound himself in the same way. Have a really noisy session sometimes – banging saucepans, stamping feet, blowing mouth organs, turning up the record player and singing as well.

- that sounds can be *the same but different*. Play about with variations on the same sound: a voice can be high or low, loud or soft, for instance – see if he can imitate you in *'whisper, whisper, whisper'*, 'SHOUT, SHOUT, SHOUT!' Or change from a tiny tapping noise to a loud banging noise. Xylophones give different notes, but it's just as much fun to try how a spoon sounds tapped on ten different objects. One father strung up different sized empty tins for banging (make sure there are no sharp edges) – bottles with different amounts of water in them are marvellous if you can be sure your child won't break them. Try scratching or finger-flicking different surfaces. Let him stir, in three separate bowls, dried peas, rice and sugar – and notice the different sounds (if he can understand well enough, you can develop this into guessing games).

- that *voices can imitate* other sounds. Parents naturally imitate the sneezes and coughs of their small children – and it's good that they do, because this teaches the child to imitate in turn. We do it with other things too – for lots of children, 'brrrm-brrrm' is their first 'word'. Extend this deliberately – say 'bang' loudly when you hear one, imitate the washing machine, the cat or dog, a creaking door, the 'ssshhh' of a fast-flowing tap and the gurgle of the water going down the plughole – and encourage your child to do it too.

- that sounds *have direction*. He needs to be able to locate sound – try asking *him* (with exaggerated questioning looks!) where everyday sounds (motor-bike, ice-cream bell, barking) are coming from – if he understands joking, look in all the unlikely places till he shows you. Make a game of rustling a sweet paper behind him and to one side – he gets the sweet if he turns in the right direction. Go and look for a heard sound together – cat, lawnmower, road drill. With the help of one or two other people, you can make games of listening for and locating a sound quite complicated.

- that sounds *are meaningful*. Talk about and demonstrate what messages different sounds are conveying to you. When you hear clinking milk bottles, a car arriving, the doorbell, the baby crying, rain, footsteps, letters on the mat, the telephone – try to make him listen with you a moment first, *then* say what it is, *then* let him see you react to what it means (or let him react himself – fetch the letters, for instance). If he's reached

the guessing-game stage, have three different noise-producing things on
the table (say, saucepan and lid, two spoons, two tins) and let him 'hide his
eyes' and guess which made the noise – or let him make *you* guess.

HELPING A CHILD TO LOOK

We want him to realise

- that *looking is interesting*. From the start, have bright moving objects in
  the room to catch his attention: mobiles that sway in any light draught
  (and perhaps tinkle as well), paper windmills, flags and streamers within
  sight when he's outside, or a leafy tree to look at if there is one. Look *with*
  him: at bedtime, make a point of playing with a look-at toy just before you
  put him down – perhaps a musical roundabout or pop-up toy – or have a
  conversation with your reflections in a mirror, or look through a picture-
  book. Make a collection of scraps that are exciting to look at – not necessarily pictures, but interesting patterns, metallic paper with reflective
  surfaces, bits of glittery or shimmery material and so on – stick them into a
  cardboard book or plastic album, or keep them in a box, and make it a bit
  of a treat to go through them with him.

- that *exploring by looking* is worth his while. Try to prevent him dropping
  or throwing a toy; he needs to look long enough to find out what's interesting about this one. 'Talk him round' the toy, helping him to discover its
  most attractive features; make sure he's looking at the moment the action
  takes place! If there's some sort of climax or moment of success,
  emphasise it with your own exclamations of enthusiasm or praise – make
  him feel it was his success, even if it was mostly yours. That will make it
  worth his while to have another go, looking more carefully this time.

- that he can *find what he wants* by looking. Don't just put a toy in his hands
  and leave it at that – encourage him to make a choice from two or three, so
  that he looks from one to another. While he's looking at a toy he likes,
  cover it with a cushion and encourage him to find it – help him by giving
  him a peep if necessary. Peep-bo and hide-and-seek games of all sorts will
  help him look. Use containers of all kinds – boxes with and without lids,
  paper bags, old handbags, a cloth bag with an elasticated opening – to put
  toys in for him to search for.

- that *pictures represent objects*. Put pictures on walls where he can see
  them (and talk to him about them), but choose them carefully – they
  should be clear pictures of familiar things. Avoid cartoon-like drawings
  and fussy designs that are difficult to see – some alphabet friezes and photo
  posters are especially good. The same applies to picture-books – look for
  clear card books early on (better than cloth). Cut pictures from catalogues
  for a talk-about scrap-book. Make an object–picture matching game – find
  pictures of simple objects, stick them on a card, and match them as closely

as you can with actual objects (we did this with a key, comb, nail, toy car, toy elephant, cotton reel, paint brush, beads, fork, spoon) – show the child the picture and let him find the object (perhaps out of only three to start with). Make him a photo cube (or little album) with photos of the people he knows best, and talk about them while he looks at it.

- that some things are *like each other*, some different. Look for toys that involve matching – colour to colour, shape to shape, size to size (your toy library will help you with a variety of these). In the kitchen, in the street, in the park, point out same and different: a big spoon and a little spoon; one blue car and another blue car just the same; here's a daisy, that's a butter-cup, here's *another* buttercup. Match pictures together – either from old catalogues, or ready-made from a game of 'snap'.

HELPING A CHILD TO USE HIS SENSE OF SMELL

We want him to realise

- that smells have *variety*. Comment on the different smells that you come across during the day, nice or less so! Use gestures as well to show that you're noticing smells – hold or twitch your nose, make a 'Bisto kid' face. Remember that he may like smells that you don't, and vice versa – there's a lot of disagreement among different people about the smells of petrol, strong cheese, tube trains, tobacco – and lots of people like their own body smells even if they dislike other people's. So don't force smell preferences on him, even if you have to try to put him off dabbling in the loo or worse!
- that he can *sniff at smells voluntarily*. Most children get mixed up about sniffing and blowing – help him by finding him interesting things to sniff and by play-acting yourself. Offer him a variety of smells – creosoted wood, fragrant leaves bruised in your fingers, cinnamon, ginger and curry, sour milk, vinegar, suede. Obviously, don't actually let him play with things he might eat or spill, but don't let necessary restrictions cut him off altogether from these sensory experiences.
- that smells have *meaning*. Often we identify a situation first by its smell – for instance, that the toast's burning or someone's filled his nappy! Share these and other meanings with your child – 'The milk's gone sour', 'There's a bonfire somewhere', 'Dinner's nearly ready', 'Daddy's made coffee', 'Jane's painting her room'. Help him also to recognise the charac-teristic smells of common objects – orange, lemon, soap, cocoa, onion and so on. One mother made a 'box of smells' to amuse her child – she sewed inside small muslin bags such 'smellies' as an old perfume bottle, cloves, a tea-bag, coal tar soap, dried orange peel, peppermint and a tobacco tin – some children would enjoy guessing at the smells, others would just like sniffing at them.

HELPING A CHILD TO TOUCH AND FEEL

We want him to realise
- that the things in the world have *many different characteristics* that he can discover by reaching out and touching. They can be hard, soft, cold, warm, wet, dry, furry, soggy, prickly, springy, powdery, hairy, smooth, rough, jagged, crumbly, holey, crackly, long, short, heavy, light, wobbly, mobile, firm, thin, thick, big, little, tall, short, bumpy, sticky, alive, flexible, stiff, round, hollow, flat, hinged, leaved, many-sided, many-parted, pourable, stirrable, silky, scratchy, spongy, velvety, slimy – and combinations of these. There are fifty 'feeling' words here, and if you think of an object to fit each of these words you will already have a variety of touch experiences for your child – yet if you walk round your kitchen or into a garden, you will find many more objects which aren't fully described by these words.
- that touch has *meaning* – it tells us something about what can be done with an object. Round things roll, prickly and spiky things may hurt if we press them too hard, sticky things leave their stickiness on our hands, and so on. Later he may learn about the combinations of characteristics that make some things float, some sink, some break, some fold and so on. Blind children will have to learn which are the important things to feel *for*, and which mere decoration. As before – offer the child the experience, talk about it (even if he doesn't understand all you say), demonstrate it.
- that hand and finger touch gives better information if we *handle things delicately*. Some children have no midway between clutching and throwing. They have to learn to hold and turn things gently in the fingers if they are to use hand and eye together; they must hold in one hand and touch with the other to explore and use toys effectively. Sometimes this itself has to be taught, perhaps by the kind of methods we have talked about earlier. Once he's got the idea, try making a 'feely bag' (see page 87).
- that there is *enjoyment* to be got from hand and finger touch. Some children love to finger a raised pattern, or stroke their mother's hair or their father's beard, or to feel his stubbly chin. Encourage this sensuous feeling – they are learning to touch gently, and to think about what they are touching.
- that there is pleasure and excitement to be found in *whole-body touch experiences*. Such experiences might be: being snuggled and rough-handled in a warm towel after a bath; splashing in the bath, or in a swimming pool (ask your toy library to consider lending special swimming aids); kicking about in a pile of dead leaves, or in hay; standing in a high wind; being thrown in the air; rolling down a grassy hill or on heather; bouncing on a trampoline or inflatable; riding a merry-go-round or a pony; swings, slides and see-saws. Some of these experiences can be frightening; if the

child is nervous, don't insist on them (the point is that he should *enjoy* them!) but try to see what is scaring him and how you could reassure him and bring back the fun. The great value of these experiences is not just that they are exciting, but that the child usually *shares* his excitement with other people: they are therefore likely to help his social and communication development.

HELPING A CHILD TO THINK ABOUT TASTES

Taste is a sense which is more difficult to talk about on its own than the other senses. This is partly because it's so mixed up with the idea of actually eating that we find it hard to separate it from how we feel about that. The child may associate the sense of taste with mealtime battles, and so may we – and for most of us this is the worst kind of battle, because as parents we probably feel that our most important duty is to nourish our child.

As well as this, the sense of taste is mixed up with other senses. Obviously it's closely allied to smell, as we soon find if we lose our sense of smell with a head cold. Also, though, it is affected by the feel and texture of food – for instance, a child may hate eggs or jelly or tapioca because the feel of them is disgusting to him, or he may eat anything crunchy however it tastes, including earth! The look of food also affects how we perceive its taste, which is why good cooks take care to make food look appetising in colour and form; children with little sight, in fact, are very often a problem to feed because there is no visual interest in their food.

We do want our child to find mealtimes enjoyable (and we want to enjoy them too). We've discussed this already in Chapter 6. We would also like him to accept a varied diet, partly because it's much easier to cope with children who aren't faddy, but also because we know that this could give him a lot of pleasure.

Obviously your child may have certain diet restrictions because of his condition. Having checked carefully on that, try to offer as wide a range of tastes as you can. For instance, does he regularly taste things in all the categories of sweet, salty, sour, bitter, bland? Do you make a game of trying out tiny tastes on his tongue as you cook, so that he learns about the flavour of the ingredients separately? Do you only offer him tastes of sweet things, or do you try to make him adventurous by offering him a strong, unusual taste, on the tip of your finger maybe, when you've got something different out – anchovy, olives, seafood? Even faddy children can surprise you!

If he *is* already faddy, check with your doctor how much he needs of the things he does not like, and whether he needs any vitamin or mineral supplements, perhaps added to his favourite drink. Once you know he's getting enough, however eccentric his diet may be, you can relax, stop pressing him to eat, and concentrate just on broadening his range of tastes. Try tiny amounts of finger foods like raisins, dried apricots, potato rings, bits of raw fruit and vegetables and so on – perhaps leave them around on saucers or paper cake cases for him to nibble from during the afternoon. Sometimes using a morsel of food as a prize for something can make a child think it *must* be nice, and even convince himself that it is. Or a little competition can work wonders; if there's no big sister to say '*I* want that raisin', try using a glove puppet to go after the raisin with great drama – just too late, you hope!

Don't forget that tastes rejected in one texture may well be accepted in another; or something he doesn't like warm might be fine just out of the fridge. Some children reject any new food on principle: if you can manage a rule that anyone has a right to refuse food *once they've tasted it*, this helps a lot. Sometimes a bit of magic like a special spoon or special cup will help the child to accept what he's offered in them.

Finally, unlike tired mums and dads, children usually like eating what they've made themselves, and cooking can be one of the most successful forms of play, even for children who don't play much in other ways. We'll give you some ideas for this in the 'So what now?' section at the end of the next chapter.

8 Play: solving the problems

In the last chapter we saw that, for all children, opportunities for experiment and exploration in play are an important part of their developmental progress. Play is certainly more than just amusement; it contributes to many different areas of a child's growth – social, intellectual, physical and emotional. Difficulties in play can hinder development in those areas. In this chapter, we will look at how certain kinds of handicap create particular problems for the child's play development; and we will think about the kinds of planning by which we might compensate for this.

In many of the examples we shall be discussing, our main concern will be to find ways of *rearranging the child's world* so that opportunities are brought within his grasp – maybe literally within the grasp of his hand, but also within the grasp of his understanding or attention. Here we are trying to make it possible for him to get the same sort of pleasure from exploring and experimenting, within the limits of his handicap, as other children do.

Most children *naturally* find play enjoyable and worthwhile. However, there are some children who don't seem to understand that play might be fun; and these are the ones whose parents are most likely to think they *cannot* play. With these children, we may have to begin by teaching them to *want* to play. Sometimes the best way to do this is to take the behavioural approach that we looked at earlier, in order to teach the child that play is worth his while.

It seems odd to talk about having to *teach* a child that play is fun – you might think every child would know that, and that if they didn't they couldn't be taught. But think of the child who will not look at a toy for more than a second, or who throws objects the moment he sees them. These children cannot seem to 'stay with' the toy long enough to find out its possibilities: how can they know that playing with it is fun, if they have never given the toy enough attention to make it 'work' for them? With such a child, then, we may start by using small rewards when he just looks at the toy, holds it without throwing, or manipulates its parts. We are helping him to give the toy a chance; and we hope that playing with the toy will become rewarding in its own right, as he experiences success with it.

Perhaps it will be useful at this point to give examples of different kinds of handicap, and the problems they pose for the child's play.

CHILDREN WITH VERY POOR VISION

Sighted babies are excited by the things they see. Soon they want what they see, and reach for it. If it is too far away, they wriggle and swivel, and shunt themselves forward, continually checking that the object is still there, still *in sight*. Much of the child's play with objects happens because of this visual excitement; and much of his early mobility is stimulated by 'I see, I want, I can get'.

Once the child has the object, he explores it to find out whether it's worth playing with; and in the process, he finds out what things can be used for, how they can be used *together* and so on, through more and more complex chains of exploration and discovery.

The child with poor vision lacks the simple starting-point of finding objects visually attractive. With no clear visual image to tempt him to reach out and move forward, he is likely to turn inward on himself. The hazy world beyond his own skin seems full of confusion. If he does move around, things come out of that world and bump him painfully; if he rolls a ball or tosses his rattle, he may never find them again – they are swallowed up in the haze. So instead of using toys in relation to his surroundings – banging, rolling, bouncing and visually exploring possibilities – the child tends to act like a much younger baby, rubbing the toy on his cheek, licking and biting it. He may cling to it so tightly, for fear of losing it, that he cannot manipulate the toy sensitively with his fingers and explore it that way. Not only are his eyes without sight, but he has what are sometimes called 'blind hands' also.

This all adds up to a very unnatural sort of play, with very limited opportunities for learning. It must be our job both to tempt the child out of this 'inward-looking' isolation, and at the same time to organise his surroundings so that he can become more confident and begin to develop the skills of exploring and finding out.

It can be a good idea to plan a part of the room in which the furniture makes a natural 'small world' in which he can feel comfortable – where settee, armchair, coffee-table perhaps, are always in the same place so that he can easily get his bearings. Within that area, it may be useful to have a smaller 'nest' still, where he can expect to find the same things each time he feels for them – one corner of the settee, a clothes basket or grocery box, perhaps his special rug with cushions around it to stop things rolling away. And we will *not* have the radio turned up all the time – the blind child needs to use his ears to listen to our footsteps, to the cat's paw-steps, to the different sounds made by himself with his playthings, and to all the creaks and rustles and chinks that tell him what's going on in his world. When he listens, he's learning.

In choosing toys, we must pay special attention to how they sound and feel. We look for interesting textures and shapes; toys with a sounding part that can be felt for as well as heard (like a bell in a cage); *different* sounds; fit-together toys which do not depend on sight. We must think about size: too small a toy car, and it may be difficult to feel details which a sighted child could easily see; a fit-together circle of plastic track may not be appreciated as a circle if it is much wider than the child's reach (whereas a sighted child could 'take in' a much bigger circle visually). With very young children, we may find it useful to anchor a series of rattles and other toys on strings, and deliberately to include one or two *pairs* of objects which the child can use together (drum and drumstick, for instance). Later, a play-overall with pockets is useful, for keeping track of small objects; or a box with compartments so that the child can feel in command of his possessions and become less dependent on others.

CHILDREN WITH VERY LITTLE MOBILITY

While the blind child is at risk of low mobility because he lacks the confidence and skills, many physically handicapped children are more permanently immobilised. For a different reason, the child cannot go after the objects around him; but at least he knows they are there. This in itself may make him very frustrated.

It would be unrealistic to say that we can ever completely prevent our child's physical difficulties from affecting his opportunities to explore and learn. What we must do is to try to understand just what he is missing by being immobile, and compensate as far as we can.

For instance, what exactly can he see from his usual position? Is it mainly blank wall, or is there a perspective, with people moving about both near and further away? How often are his position and view changed? Is he *high* enough to interact easily with people passing? More important for play, are there toys near his hands (or feet), are they of the sort that he can make work by a kick or a shove, are they too close for his eyes to focus on? A beach ball or balloon on a string may be good for kicking – so may bells or rattles on a piece of elastic. A small movement may take immense physical effort: we must look for toys that give very rewarding responses for the child's purposeful movement. Where the child's problem is uncontrolled movement rather than lack of movement, we have to ensure that the whole toy is not sent flying by a jerking arm as the child tries to carry out a controlled action.

Never be reluctant to ask questions of the physiotherapist and occupational therapist at your hospital, *whether or not you are seeing them regularly*; it's their job to get these things right for your child. Some questions cannot be usefully answered in general terms, without seeing the individual child. How can he be positioned or propped in order to get the visual distance right and to give his arms the right degree of support for maximum effectiveness? What can he be taught to do when his fingers lock? How can he be helped to bring his hands together? Which sitting, kneeling or standing supports will give him most 'play-power', and with what kind of table? Can he use a special trike, a swing or a baby-walker, and what kind, or with what modifications? What shoes will help his mobility? These are not questions that can be answered here, but they are examples of those you need to put to the hospital therapists.

In trying to help a child with poor mobility to play, we must try to compensate for his physical *helplessness*. A lot of the time he is dependent on us to bring things to him; we should try to find ways for him to reach for or pull in objects for himself. We should not just operate toys ourselves to amuse the child; we should deliberately look for ways he can make things happen for himself. Obviously he will enjoy our involvement in his play and this is important for his social development. But we should also be looking for things which give the child some *power* over his play environment, and the opportunity to learn about relationships between things ('If I pull this string, that happens'; 'If I bang this and this together, I get *that* noise').

As we've seen before, learning takes place more quickly if the learner is *active*. The word 'feedback' is a useful idea to bear in mind – the idea that the child will learn more effectively if he *sees and hears the results* of his own actions. A well-placed mirror may help; so may toys that make sounds on contact; toys that move easily (perhaps a balloon tied to a child's wrist or ankle for a short while); swinging or teetering toys that move with a clumsy swipe; or some of the new battery or electronic toys – all of these give feedback and therefore a sense of achievement to the child.

Another problem for the immobile child is that he is often cut off from the range of bodily sensations which other children discover just by 'getting into everything'. Normal children experience the feel and smell of dirt and earth, the undersides of hedges, the insides of neglected cupboards, the bath plughole, drains, car wheels, as well as many more acceptable sensations; we tend to protect physically handicapped children from these experiences, and to make their lives more sterile than they need be. Perhaps we should think harder about how to vary the child's experience – let him lie on grass (not just a rug), touch earth and mud and pastry and spaghetti, feel warm and cold trickles of water, rough surfaces as well as smooth, prickly as well as soft. Beanbags, inflatable toys, dry leaves, packaging materials, can all be useful in expanding a child's experience. Don't forget that just *because* your child is used to only a narrow range of experiences, he may be nervous when you introduce new ones. Never force him, don't feel disappointed, but wait until a better moment and try again gently and calmly.

CHILDREN WHO ARE SLOW LEARNERS

Ordinary children are led on in their play by the excitement of their own thoughts. They look at a toy and at once all sorts of questions come into their minds: What's this for? What could I do with it? What will happen if I do *this* – or *that*? When they try out these questions, what does happen will suggest more ideas to them, and so their exploration becomes more and more complicated.

For the mentally handicapped child, the interesting questions don't so easily come to mind, and they don't so easily lead on to further ideas. The child's activity with a toy may come to a full stop, because his thoughts have come to a full stop. At this point, instead of continuing to look at and explore the toy, he may drop it or throw it aside – CRASH! – and suddenly he's done something interesting. This is one way the child with limited ideas may learn to throw toys as his *main* activity with them, and this in turn prevents him keeping the toy in his hands long enough to find out about more adventurous possibilities for play with it.

Some children who find the world particularly confusing and disturbing – autistic children, for instance – take refuge in one or two rather narrow forms of play. This seems to make them feel safer because it has become so familiar – the child twiddles a piece of string, folds and unfolds paper, or spins objects, for instance. At the same time, though, it has the effect of shutting off the child's attention from other possible interesting activities. Some children develop an obsessive interest in one or two play activities – setting out lines of objects, for instance, or searching for particular patterns in everything – and again, this seems to close their minds to real exploratory play.

When a child seems to have 'got stuck' in his play – as if he isn't aware of the next possibilities – start thinking about what he seems to find rewarding now, and how you could build on that. Is it a particular kind of sound he enjoys? Show him other ways of producing similar kinds of sounds, help him to try out new sound-making activities, gradually increase the variety and introduce him to rhythm and pitch, encouraging him to use his body in time with the sound. Perhaps he loves throwing? By your close involvement, encourage him to build higher before knocking down the pile, make him soft bean bags to throw into a clothes basket (so that throwing becomes aiming), try a sound (bell, animal noise) in the bag to encourage him to listen as well as throw.

8 Play: solving the problems

It's not always a matter of enlarging on a child's play. With some children, one gets the feeling that things are so confused and chaotic for them that what they most need is someone to make things calm and very simple. For a child like this, a quiet room and a patient adult who will lead him through the possibilities of *one toy at a time* are most helpful – a rich variety only confuses him all the more.

All through our discussion of play, we have emphasised the importance of the parent who plays *with* the child. He doesn't need your involvement in every minute of his play, nor will he always want it. He does need to be started off, and to be helped to keep going and move onward, much more than ordinary children. And one enormous advantage most of us find, as we play with our handicapped child, is that we become better and better at seeing things from his point of view. This above all will teach us ways of making play more rewarding to him, and therefore a richer learning experience.

So what now?

We originally intended to make a list of especially useful toys at this point, with notes on how they could help a handicapped child. However, the many toy libraries that now exist keep their own very good (and up-to-date) lists of toys, and are likely to have what is probably the most comprehensive and useful list of all: the *ABC of Toys*, published by the Toy Libraries Association and regularly updated in new editions. You should also be able to get the ABC through your local public library, if there is no toy library near you.

So it seems most useful now to think about what you can do *without* bought toys. Toys help, but often the most interesting kind of play comes from parents (and the rest of the family) using their ingenuity and involvement.

LAP PLAY

Some of the earliest communication-through-play happens when the child is on your lap or cuddled up close beside you. We'll be looking at language in the next chapter; meanwhile remember that communication is not just through speaking – it also comes through smiles, laughter, frowns, hugs, gesture and any sort of touch.

When he sits close to you, and you look through a book or illustrated catalogue together, you are communicating, even if he doesn't understand your speech. Point to the picture; help him to point too. Once again, use your face like an actor; show astonishment by opening your eyes wide and saying 'Ooooh!'; draw a breath, 'Aaah!'; look at a picture of food and smack your lips; shut your eyes and snore for 'sleepy', and so on.

Try action games on your knee with the old rhymes: 'This little piggy went to market', 'Round and round the garden', 'Pat-a-cake', 'Horsie Horsie', 'This is the way the lady rides'. These are good because both the words and the actions become so familiar and remind the child of each other. Action rhymes also give the child a sense of anticipation and sequence – the 'I know what's coming next' feeling – and this helps him to feel he's in control, and encourages his ability to concentrate on a series of actions. Finger games take this further, helping both imitation and hand–eye co-ordination. If you've forgotten the words and actions, cheap and helpful books are suggested on page 126.

A few children, especially those who are somewhat autistic, refuse to sit on a lap if it means looking at their parent's face. If your child is like this, don't give up lap play; turn your child with his back to you (either on your lap or on the settee beside you) and bring your hands in front of him to do the actions. In time he may tolerate facing you more closely in order to get a rhyme he has come to like. Children who dislike communication still need it – more than most!

Try 'talking games' with a toy telephone, if you have one; or use the tube from a roll of kitchen paper, bent over at the end, to represent the receiver. Draw faces on your finger ends (not the nail side) with a ballpoint, and make your fingers into little men to talk to the child – draw them on his fingers too, and let his little men talk back. In these talking games, it doesn't matter if you can't fully understand each other, because you've got the fun of the actions to carry you along. If you're really ambitious, embroider little people on each finger of a glove for a whole family of finger puppets. Remember that the faces should be on the *inside* so that they can bend for lots of movement. You can even dress them – make the thumb the baby, so that the others can bend over it!

BATH AND WATER PLAY

As soon as possible, get your baby used to water. Let him lie on a nappy in about 1½ inches of warm water in the big bath, while you kneel on the floor and talk to him, lapping the water against him and trickling it from the sponge. Don't soap him for a few minutes – let him get used to turning his head and getting clean warm water in ears, eyes and mouth.

Once he's sitting, he's got to feel safe and stable to enjoy it. A towel to sit on is just as effective as a special non-slip mat. However, he may still be wobbly. If he seems to need something to hang on to, sit him in a plastic clothes basket inside the bath (this may have the additional advantage that you can bath another more able child at the same time – and the water can be the right depth for each child).

It's nice to have boats, ducks and fish to float in the water; but there are lots of water toys which give just as much pleasure and cost little or nothing. Make a collection and hang it in a string bag on the tap, so he can see and choose.

Clean squeezy bottles are obviously fun – have one with the nozzle pulled out, for pouring, and one with it left in for squirting (you may have to fill it for him). A plastic jug fills much more easily, and he can put things inside it. An old ball is fun – he can press it on to the floor of the bath and watch it pop up. A cork tile, perhaps cut smaller, makes a kind of floating table. Plastic funnels are even better if they have a foot of rubber tubing attached. An old metal teapot with a lid, and a beaker to pour into, adds make-believe play, especially if you keep a vinyl doll in the bath to make the tea for. Plastic straws are nice – he'll probably drink less bath water through them than straight from the bath or flannel, he can blow air-bubbles in the water, and a handful makes good flotsam for him to pick from the water straw by straw.

Two or three teaspoons are also good for slowing up his water intake, and are a challenge to pick off the bottom of the bath. A softly-inflated balloon bobs about pleasantly – nice for two children together. A string of wooden or plastic beads can be put in and out of things, or even worn! A paper bag only lasts one bathtime, but can be a lot of fun until it falls apart.

If you do want to buy a bath toy, two of the best are Kiddicraft's Bath Ducks and Wobble Globe. The three ducks (different colours) are hollow, can be used for pouring as well as floating, and will hook themselves together, beak to tail, for formation swimming! The wobble globe is a transparent ball on a rubber stem which fixes to the bathside by suction-pad; it contains coloured beads, and what gives this version the edge over other makes is that it can be unscrewed to half-fill with water – which not only makes it extra interesting as a rattle, but allows the beads to bob about in quite a different way. If you don't want to spend the money, you can make almost as good a toy out of a transparent plastic bottle of the kind that cooking oil or squash often comes in. Wash it well with detergent, and *press* in beads, bottle caps or other objects that won't come out again. Then you can give it to the child without a lid, so that he can use it either as a rattle, or with water in to shake, and watch the floating objects bobbing.

MESSY PLAY

Water

Besides the things he can do *in* the bath, a bowl of water on the grass (or a sinkful in the kitchen) may give him longer to play because you don't have to stay beside him. With a little washing-up liquid and a piece of tubing, he can blow frothy piles of bubbles. Bubbles blown through a bubble-wand are also better out of the bath, because most children want to try and catch them as they float, and that's likely to cause slipping in the bath. If you have a garden, there's all the delight of a hose shower in the summer; but even a balcony or yard will allow him to use a small watering can. It's also surprising how few handicapped children ever get the chance to wash up, and how many of them can do at least some of it quite well, with a little helpful supervision – and what an achievement!

Dough

Commercial modelling doughs and clays are expensive, especially for a clumsy child who needs good big lumps. Make your own: mix a tablespoon of cooking oil and half a cup of water, stir in two cups of flour and three-quarters of a cup of salt. Work this into a dough with your hands – you might need a little more water. Colour half with food colouring if you like. This dough is for squeezing, rolling and making marks in, rather than for real modelling, but it's unlikely that the child is at the modelling stage anyway. Provide tools for pressing and making marks – lollysticks, cotton reels, an old ballpoint, large button, or anything else suitable and safe for your child to have.

This dough will last for several days if you keep it in the fridge or other cool place in a plastic bag.

Paint

Bought finger paints are very expensive and soon get used up; paint boxes are usually too fiddly. It's worth buying three large bottles of ready-mixed water paint (gouache) in red, blue and yellow, from which you can mix your own purple, orange, green and brown – they may seem expensive, but they'll last ages. Thicken up the paint with a little 'tapwater' paste from the ironmonger's – and you've got finger paints. Old saucers or patty pans are easier for the child to manage than more tippy containers like yoghurt pots. The best place for this activity is probably the floor, covered with lots of newspaper; if you haven't got cover-up overalls for the child, an old shirt with the sleeves cut short and string round the waist is a very good substitute. Don't expect real pictures – the child is literally 'making his mark', and it's enough for him just to create an effect. You might like to try the reverse process: brush the paste-and-paint thickly all over the paper and let the child draw patterns in this with his fingers – or make a 'comb' with a piece of card, and let him draw patterns with that. Don't forget to praise him, show the rest of the family, and pin his efforts up somewhere for him to be proud of.

COOKING

Most parents, when they think of cooking with a child, think 'pastry'. This is not only a lot of trouble, but too difficult for many children. However, most handicapped children can cook if you choose something suitable and give them help. The satisfaction of making something that not only they but the rest of the family can eat with pleasure beats most other kinds of play!

For instance, most children can stir up an instant whip and scatter chocolate dots on top, with help if necessary. Most can put fillings on to ready sliced and buttered bread for sandwiches. Many can mash or chop a banana, whip cream or dream topping with a rotary whisk and combine them. Again with help, little iced cakes made from a packet mix are really exciting to cook: an egg is stirred into the mix, spooned into the paper cases provided, and after cooking a water icing is mixed and spread, and decorations added, all from one packet. The skills the child learns from this are many – opening the packet, pouring out without spilling, pouring water, stirring, spooning accurately, spreading, placing decorations – and of course you will later be able to use such activities to add measuring, counting, even skilled egg-breaking, as well as all the talk that it can involve.

We've been cooking with mentally handicapped children of different ages and abilities for some years, and we love it because of all the opportunities we've listed here, because it can be organised to exactly suit a child's level, but most of all because the children themselves love it so much. With a group of children, the least able can cook plums and instant whip, the middling ones can make little cakes and the old hands will be on to shepherd's pie or even pastry – and a whole meal made by such a group is appreciated as a wonderful achievement by everyone. The important thing in achieving this kind of success for less able children is to have a helper for each child. To see a hyperactive child *carefully* decorating 'his' blancmange and *slowly* carrying it to the table is a thrill for anyone who knows such a child.

SOME THINGS TO MAKE

A personal scrapbook

The kind of achievement that the child discovers in cooking can be multiplied in value if you keep a scrapbook for him. Draw or photograph his cake or pudding – preferably let him be making it in the picture – and stick it in his book. If you have an instant camera, that makes a tremendous impact for the child, because the record of his achievement comes out of the camera there and then, without the endless wait of processing (when he's likely to forget the whole thing anyway). This is what's called eating your cake and having it!

Scrapbooks like these, in which the child himself is hero of the story, make a wonderful focus for conversation with the child, even if he can't talk himself. They also keep his best memories alive, which is a very difficult thing for a child with poor language. We've mentioned such scrapbooks in connection with cooking because this has produced some of the favourite achievements of children we know – but of course a scrapbook can record memories of many different activities. 'Phyllis swinging very high', 'Richard not being frightened of a dog', 'Debbie playing a tune', 'Mark listening', 'Andrea washing up', 'Wayne putting his socks on' – these are all achievements which we have photographed for children's scrapbooks. Scrapbooks can also include all sorts of other things – tickets, sweet wrappers, picture cards, postcards, and even bumpy things like shells, stones, twigs and other objects that the child has taken pleasure in collecting – anything will do, so long as it means something to the child and can be made to stick!

Something to wear

Earlier on, we mentioned a play overall with lots of pockets for a blind child. For any child it might be fun to make a play-garment with nteresting things sewn all over it (probably a tabard shape – simple back and front, with a hole in the middle for the head – would be most practical). It could have bells on the hem, patches of pretty material such as lurex, brocade and velvet; pockets from which would emerge, on short cords so as not to get lost, a tiny teddy, a peg doll, a plastic or metal mirror; shiny buttons and beads sewn on in patterns; embroidered pictures (you could buy patches if you can't embroider – but try a train, with buttons for wheels); nylon ribbon streamers; perhaps a whistle; and anything else that turns up and is safe (often things that used to be attached to key fobs are suitable). Another thing that some children love is hats, and a carrier bag full of hats can be a favourite toy – it is usually easy to collect a few very cheaply (look in jumble sales, ask your friends), and you can brighten them up with bits of ribbon, buttons and bells.

Feely bags and boxes

This is one way of helping the child to think about what he feels. You can either use a cardboard box with two holes cut in the side for the child to put his arms into; or, more comfortable, make a closed bag, about as big as a cushion cover, with a slit in each end. You put any familiar object in the bag – toothbrush, cotton reel, comb, matchbox, toy car, plastic mug are examples – and get the child to feel it with both hands until he recognises it. If he can talk, encourage him to name it; if not, just wait for the look of recognition, then let him take it out to check.

Another, more difficult kind of feely bag, for a child who can talk quite well, is the sort where a whole lot of different objects are each sewn into its own soft cotton bag – this takes very little time if you've got a sewing machine. The child feels each object through the cotton, talking about how it feels, and guesses what it is. This game only works for a child who is happy to name the object and check by having another feel, because he's not going to be able to get at the object itself – unless you go to the trouble of putting press studs or velcro on the bags; and that might be worth doing, because you could then change the objects around.

9 First steps towards language

In the last two chapters we looked in a general way at play. One major point was left out of those chapters which we might have included: play situations are an important part of how a child learns to use and develop *language*. This chapter will look more closely at the complicated business of learning language, and we shall be particularly geared towards children who have little or no language.

If you were asked to describe what language is, what would you say? The chances are that terms like 'speech', 'words', 'sentences' and 'communication' would quickly spring to mind. Well, what about sign language? What about smiling, nodding, pointing or waving – do they count as language? Certainly they are used to *communicate meaning* – that is, to tell another person about feelings, intentions, facts and so on, in the same way that spoken words are.

It is important to realise that *language means more than just speech*, and more than the simple pronouncing of words. *It is something we use to let other people know what we mean.* Speech is the main form, but not the only form of language; and spoken words just repeated parrot-fashion are not language (within our definition) unless the speaker both understands their meaning and intends to pass on that meaning to the listener.

Perhaps we should pause at once to think about the differences between speech and language. For most of us, speech has a central place in our everyday lives. It is important for us both to understand and to be able to use speech; because this is by far the most convenient method of sharing our thoughts with other human beings.

Some people can understand speech without being able to use it. No one can use speech *spontaneously* – that is, making it up for themselves as they go along, not 'parrotting' someone else – without being able to understand it. However, a child may repeat or echo words, or even sentences, without understanding their meaning. These are, as we shall see, important points to remember when we are considering a handicapped child.

So it would be wrong to think that the statement 'My child has no speech' means the same as 'My child has no language'. To have no language would mean (a) that he does not understand either words or gesture; and (b) that he has no symbolic way of communicating his needs and intentions (we will look at the word 'symbolic' in a minute).

A child may have his own 'language' (double-dutch or signs) which may or may not involve 'words', and may or may not be understood by many other people. People who know him best do recognise it as a language because he uses the *same* sounds or gestures consistently to mean the same thing, and gradually they may be able to share it with him. Obviously a language that is only understood by the child and one or two others is not so convenient as a language which is shared by most of the people around him. But it still is language, and in the case of a child who seems unlikely ever to achieve normal spoken language, or to speak at all, it is something we should feel able to work with, or towards, optimistically.

Unfortunately in this chapter we will not have the space to explore the practical use of sign language. In fact, the actual teaching of language to a handicapped child is more than we can go into in depth in this book. Here we will concentrate on the very beginnings of language and speech. If your child is ready to move on, you will need one of the books which have been written to help you more fully in this special area, and which we list at the end.

To sum up our first points, then: language is the way we communicate what we mean; but language is not necessarily in the form of speech, nor is speech necessarily language.

SYMBOLS

The use of the word 'symbolic' earlier may have seemed confusing. It is important to understand the idea that language, whether spoken or signed, consists of symbols. A symbol is *something which is understood to stand for something else*. A picture is one example of a symbol; miming or 'make believe' is another. So is language. For example, the word 'table' is not *itself* a table; it is a sound, or series of sounds, which we all (in English at any rate) agree *stands for* a particular object.

The same applies to gestures, whether it is waving goodbye, beckoning 'come on' or thumbing a lift. These are agreed and understood to symbolise (stand for) feeling or intention. You may know, though, that in some countries 'goodbye' is signalled by a gesture which looks like the one which English people would take to mean 'come here' – which can cause embarrassing moments for English people abroad! So symbols have *agreed* meaning, not built-in meanings.

Let's take another example to show the difference between an *action* and a

89

symbolic gesture. When a child reaches for a toy, this is an action – even if he doesn't succeed in grasping it. When he points at something with his forefinger, this is a symbolic gesture: he is using a simple sign to indicate the toy to someone. It may be of course, that the child's father sees his unsuccessful reaching and gets the toy for him; but this does not make his reaching a sign, because he *did not intend it as communication*. When the child points, on the other hand, he is not trying to perform the action itself, but is *trying to communicate* to his father what he wants. The distinction is important, because we will not understand what level of using symbols a child has reached unless we can tell the difference between his actions and his signs. Mimicking or *pretending* to do an action comes somewhere in between, and we'll come back to this later.

So, language is symbolic: we use sounds or gesture to get across our meaning because we know that the person we are communicating with will understand those sounds or gestures to represent particular objects, intentions, feelings and so on.

An understanding of 'symbolic representation' is something which a child has to learn. Early in life a child only knows about things that actually exist in the here and now. Babies often get distressed when people or things disappear, because to them it means that the person or object no longer exists: 'out of sight, out of existence'.

We first know that a child realises that things continue to exist, even if they're out of sight, when he looks around for a toy that has rolled away or disappeared. A well-known psychological test for young babies involves showing the baby an object which he likes, putting it on a table in front of him, then covering it with a handkerchief. Very young babies will make no attempt to search under the handkerchief; older babies will, though, and this is a sign that they have reached the stage of understanding that an object can exist even though they cannot see it. The object, while it is out of sight, has become *symbolic* for them – in other words, they have an *idea* of the object (perhaps in the form of a 'picture' in their head).

Later, children show more obvious signs of understanding the use of symbols – for example in make-believe play. They will use objects to represent something completely different (a stick can be a gun; a broomstick, a horse), or play at being someone else; or even pass each other imaginary tea and cake and pretend to eat and drink, mimicking real actions. This is called symbolic play.

You may wonder why we have spent so long looking at symbols. The answer is that using symbols is a kind of *playing with thoughts*; and being comfortable with thoughts as well as with real objects is a basic skill which a child needs to have before we can set about any language teaching. (We actually talk about 'turning a thought over in our mind' just as we talk about turning over an object in our hands in order to examine it.)

If necessary we may have to help the child to get to this point. If you are not sure whether your child has this comfortable grasp of symbols, you may need to try out some 'games' to check.

IMITATION

An ability to imitate is another important skill we all need to possess if we are to develop our language. Most children are surrounded by speech and gesture in their daily life (a psychologist once called it a 'blooming, buzzing confusion'), so they have no shortage of things to imitate. Out of this confusion they need to pick out particularly important bits to imitate – more difficult than it might seem for a child who doesn't know where one word ends and the next begins! (Suppose we read that last sentence aloud – how would a baby know that there *weren't* words like 'zuntno', 'dends' or 'nextbee'?)

Imitation of actions usually comes before imitation of sounds or words, perhaps just because actions are easier to pick out as single items. In working out whether our child is ready to develop language, we need to know not only 'Can he symbolise?' but also 'Can he imitate?' So we will ask ourselves firstly whether the child can imitate our *actions* (e.g. waving goodbye, banging a hand on the table, sticking the tongue out).

Secondly, if he has no words – can he repeat sounds we make for him (for instance, animal noises, 'nonsense' sounds, 'oo', 'puh', 'lala')? When we are checking on this, we need to make sure that our child is imitating us and not we him! – though children do in fact learn to imitate by picking up their parents' imitation of them.

If our child shows very little imitation of sounds or gestures, it may be that it is here that we shall need to concentrate our first efforts. In spoken language, we not only say the words that will communicate our intention, but we also let our voices rise and fall, get softer and louder and so on, in order to make our meaning more clear. If we try to get our child to imitate different *levels* of sounds as well as different *kinds* of sounds, we are helping him to develop another important skill – that of *listening*. An important part of both understanding and using language is the ability to attend and listen carefully enough to sort out which sounds are important and which are just background noise. (Actual hearing problems can interfere with this. If your child is deaf or hard of hearing for any reason, ask your specialist how this will affect how he *sorts out* sounds.)

Understanding language for most children comes quite some time before they can use language themselves. Before we look more closely at this, let's sum up what we have learned about what language is built upon. We've seen that the most important skills a child needs to have in order to develop language are:

91

9   First steps towards language

(1)   An understanding of symbols; this can be in the form of thinking about things that aren't actually in sight; using and understanding gestures; recognising pictures; or playing 'make-believe' games.

(2)   An ability to imitate accurately actions, gestures and sounds that are made by others.

If we have some doubts about our child's abilities in these areas, then it is here that we should begin our language activities, rather than expect anything more complicated of him just yet.

UNDERSTANDING LANGUAGE

So we should not expect our child to start using language until we are sure that he is understanding some of the language around him. This is, again, something we will need to check carefully. For example, can he understand instructions we may give him – to give us something, to fetch something, to do something, not to touch something and so on?

A common misunderstanding is to think that a child is understanding what we *say* when in fact he is understanding a gesture – or a mixture of our gestures and a familiar situation. So we may think that our child understands 'Put on your coat'; but if we are standing in the hall with our coat on and the door open, and perhaps reaching for his coat ourselves, it is difficult to know how much the actual words mean to him, compared with all the other clues (or *cues*) he is getting about what we might want. To be sure of how far he has got in language, we need to be sure of which cue he is responding to. Just what is he understanding or following? Is it our spoken language? Are we making gestures that could help him? Is it the well-practised situation?

If we are sure that our child can follow instructions, *how difficult* can these instructions be? Does our child only understand a simple request – 'Give me the sweets' (when the sweets are in sight)? Or can he cope with 'Get me the sweets; they're on the kitchen table' (in another room, but in view when he gets there)? Or, still more difficult, because both out of sight and unexpected, would he understand 'Get me the sweets; they're upstairs under my pillow'?

There are many other ways of finding out what level of speech our child responds to. At a simple level, we need to know, for example, whether he responds to his own name; recognises a particular voice; or perhaps reacts differently to a kind voice and an angry voice. At a more complex level, we might see if he can look at or point to objects or familiar people or parts of his body when we name them; or respond to words in some way which shows us that he is getting information from them – using the *words* as his cues, not the situation. We could check whether he understands when we describe where things might be in relation to other things – words like 'in', 'on', 'under', 'behind'.

It's important to understand that we are not trying to catch him out or see

92

if he's cheating. We simply need to know what cues he needs in order to understand, if we are to be able to help him properly by teaching the things he most needs to learn next so as to make progress.

Even if we are sure that our child is using symbols, and can imitate, we may still be doubtful about how much language he understands. We may need to concentrate for a while on increasing both the quantity and the quality of that understanding. *Understanding language always comes before using it properly for communication.*

This chapter has only been able to concentrate on the *basics* of language – in other words, what a child needs to master before language can develop. It has therefore been concerned mainly with children who have very little or no spoken language. Whether or not our child has any speech, to help him effectively we need to sort out in our minds exactly what we are trying to achieve – a better understanding of symbols, better imitation and so on – and then work out activities which will take us towards that particular goal. We have mentioned a few here, but once you get started you will need to be inventive yourself in thinking up activities which your own child will enjoy.

Other ideas will be found in the books we have recommended, from the professionals you are in contact with, and from your local toy library – don't be afraid to ask! Children need a *variety* of activities in order to keep them interested, and to prevent the whole thing turning into a boring drill session. The best language programmes give the child an understanding, which is continuously renewed, that language enriches his life – that it is worth his while, in fact.

For some time there is likely to be uncertainty as to just how far our child will be able to develop his language. But if we have some idea of what lies behind the learning of language, the guidelines of the behavioural approach will be useful here too:

- being clear about our aims;
- designing activities in such a way that this particular child finds them rewarding;
- carrying out our programme regularly but in small steps;
- being patient;
- recording progress;
- and, here particularly, watching our own language carefully so that we make things as simple and clear as possible for our child.

These guidelines simply help us to help our child in a systematic and organised way.

Never forget that communication is about *sharing*. It happens when parents and child play with a toy together and share the pleasure of it; or when we blow him a bubble and he pops it; or when he feeds us a biscuit and we smack our lips over it; or when we walk hand in hand with him down the street and stop to look together down a hole in the road; or when he sneezes

93

and we say 'Bless you!' and he smiles; or when he has a bounce on his mother's knee or settles down on his father's lap for a snooze. All of these things are *very important* kinds of communication, and they need very little speech – or even none at all.

But to be able to make use of language, whether spoken or signed, has all kinds of side-effects for our child – intellectual and emotional, as well as social. It enables him to communicate more effectively with his fellow human beings, and to avoid the frustration of being unable to express his wants and feelings – a frustration which can sometimes take the form of angry or panicky behaviour. There is also a definite relationship between language and thinking (cognitive development): putting thoughts into words helps people to work things out more logically, and to sort out problems themselves. If we can help our child to develop his language skills, we may well find that our efforts bring results in other areas of his development.

So what now?

OBSERVING LANGUAGE

Below are some questions to help you work out how your own child fits into the pattern of development described in Chapter 9. At the end of each set of questions, ask yourself if this is an area in which your child needs extra help.

(1) Looking for objects

> Main question: Does he always look in the most likely place to find toys which he wants or has lost?

If *yes*, go on to the questions about *imitation*.
If *no*, or you're unsure, here are some further questions:
- Will he look in the right place for an object he wants, after he's seen you cover it with a handkerchief or put it in a box?
- Will he look in the right direction for toys he's dropped, or which have rolled out of sight?
- Are there some objects which he likes better than others?
  Does he recognise them and choose them?
  Does he 'explore' them with his eyes, mouth and hands?

(2) Imitation

> Main questions:
> Can he imitate actions which you show him?
> Can he imitate new words you speak to him?

If *yes*, move on to the question about *gesture*.
If *no*, or if you're unsure, here are some more questions which may help; the first few are to do with imitating *actions*, and the later ones with imitating *sounds*.
- If you do something with a doll, toy car etc., can he imitate what you've done?
- Can he play an imitating game, like 'pat-a-cake', or bang a spoon in turn with you?

95

- Does he wave goodbye when you wave to him, or shut his eyes if you shut yours?
- Does he make sounds (babble) when you talk to him?
- Can he imitate animal sounds after you; or other noises (crying, cough, sneeze)?
- Can he imitate letter sounds: 'p', 'mm', 'd'? Is there *anything else* he imitates?
- Can he imitate any facial movements of yours – waggling your tongue, wrinkling your nose, smacking your lips?

(3) Gesture

Main question: Can he use different gestures to let you know what he wants?

If *yes*, go on to the questions about *make-believe*.
If *no*, or you're unsure, try these questions:
- Does he shake his head to mean 'no' (not just turn his head away)?
- Does he tap your hand to get your attention?
- Does he point to objects regularly in the house or out of doors (with one finger extended – not just reaching with his whole hand)?
- If you point at something, will he look in the right direction? If you point at something that's behind him, will he turn round to look?
- Does he put his arms up when he wants you to lift him up?
- Will he wave goodbye before anyone else does it?
- Is there any other gesture he uses to show you what he means – palms together under tilted head to mean sleepy, finger in mouth to mean hungry, finger on lips to mean quiet?

(4) Make-believe

Main question: Does he often act in a make-believe way – putting on a hat and 'being' someone else, perhaps – or by having 'imaginary people' in his play, or in some other similar way?

If *yes*, go on to the questions about *understanding language*.
If *no*, or if you're unsure, try the following questions:
- Does he ever use dolls *as if* they were babies – tucking them up kindly (not just dumping them in a pram and covering their faces up); or perhaps feeding them or wiping their noses?

96

- Does he run toy cars along, making 'brrm-brrm' noises for them, taking petrol and so on – or is a car just something to twiddle, from his point of view?
- In general, does he treat toys according to their different uses, and *not* just as objects for throwing, objects for biting and so on?
- Does he ever play at being asleep, or pretend to eat from an *empty* spoon or cup?
- Does he ever look at a picture and 'do the actions' – pretend to comb his hair when he sees the picture of a comb, make lip-smacking noises for a cake picture, stroke the pussy-picture, roar for the lion?
- Will he pretend to use a toy telephone?
- Is there anything else which he does in the way of 'pretend' or 'make-believe' play?

(5)   Understanding language

Main question: Does he often pay attention to, and understand, part of a conversation between you and another person?

If *yes*, go on to the final section on *spoken language*.
If *no*, or if you're unsure, try the following questions:
- Does he respond to his own name?
- Can he point to parts of the body (hand, foot, arms, legs, eyes, mouth etc.) on himself or on a doll, if you name them?
- Can he point to, or show you, familiar people or objects if you ask him to?
- Can he carry out simple instructions (for instance, 'Fetch the ball', 'Shut the door', 'Don't touch that') if you *don't* give him clues by gesturing or looking?
- Does he understand instructions to put something *in*, *on*, *under* or *behind* something else?
- Can he follow an instruction when the object is hidden – for instance, 'Get the sweets; they're in my bag'? (No clues from you!)
- Can he follow a *surprising* instruction, such as 'Get your coat; it's under my bed'?

(6)   Spoken language

Main question: Can he speak in correct, complete sentences to let you know what he means or wants?

9 First steps towards language

If *yes*, then your child is above the level of Chapter 9.

If *no*, try the following questions to see how far your child has progressed towards speaking:

- Does he seem to try out or practise sounds as if he is interested in the sound pattern – or put sounds together in strings – 'burra-burra', 'dubbly-dubbly' etc.?
- Does he use bits of words: 'b' meaning 'baby', 'n' meaning 'no', 'uh' meaning 'up' and so on?
- Has he few words, but also other sounds which he *regularly* uses to mean an object or an activity, so that you know what he is 'talking' about but others don't?
- Can he point out about 10 different objects when you say 'Where's the . . .' or 'Show me the . . .'?
- Can he *name* about 10 different objects if you point to them, or show him a picture of them, saying 'What's this?'?
- Are there ten or more words which he uses correctly and spontaneously for 'comment' (without you saying them for him to copy)?
- Does he put together two or three words to let you know what he wants or means – 'Daddy gone', 'Want crisp', 'Mummy shoe off'?
- Does he use verbs (action words) – 'eat', 'sleep', 'kick', 'fall', 'go', 'give'?
- Does he use the words 'I' or 'me', rather than his own name, in talking about his own actions or wants?
- Can he answer a question in two or three words: 'How did you hurt your knee?' – 'Jane, swing, bump', or 'Fall, on road'?
- Can he use 'wh–' words (other than 'what') to ask a question: 'Where Daddy?', 'When go out?', 'Why bed?'?

WHAT TO DO NEXT?

Once you have looked at the six sections above, you will be ready to sum up with the following three questions:

(1)   In which of these sections do you think that your child has more or less completed his development?

(2)   Which are the areas where he still has problems and needs help?

(3)   If he needs help in more than one area, which one should you concentrate on *now*? (They are more-or-less in order of normal development, so it is likely that the problem area with the lowest number is the best one to start with.)

Having answered these questions, you could turn next for further advice to any of the books we list on language development, or you could ask for local professional help (speech therapists, school etc.). The subject of language, and how it develops in children, is fairly complicated. This chapter can really only be an introduction; but at least it may set you thinking about how to move on from here.

98

10 The feelings and emotions aroused in adults by handicapped children

This chapter is rather different from the rest of the book. Until now we have been mainly focusing on the handicapped child, and thinking about how his parents can have an effect on him. Here we want to turn this around, and focus upon parents and other adults, in order to consider what effect the child has on them. Those of us who have had a handicapped child know that life is never quite the same again; and professionals too are affected by the child emotionally, in ways which they don't always want to admit. Feelings and emotions also affect how we communicate – whether we are talking about communication between parents and children, or between parents and professionals. In a book which is first and foremost about communication, we must obviously think about feelings too.

Most parents find that just having a normal child arouses emotions in them that they have not experienced before, and which may, at first, take them by surprise. Parents may be surprised at the *force* of their feelings of tenderness and protectiveness; but equally they may be taken aback to find that their child is so good at 'getting under their skin' by crying and refusing to be comforted, or by defying them, especially in public places. One mother said 'I didn't know I'd *got* a temper until I had Lawrence'; she found she could be patient and calm with other people's children, but Lawrence was able to make her feel foolish, and useless *as a mother*, in a way that was difficult to bear. Parents often use phrases like 'She shows me up' or 'He lets me down' in talking about their children's behaviour – and this shows us how all children can easily hurt their parents' pride.

If ordinary children cause unexpected emotions in their parents, how much more so will the birth of a handicapped child. Although the traditional first question at the birth is 'Is he all right?', none of us *really* expects to have a handicapped child. Very few people are prepared for such an experience in any way, and most would feel very uncertain about whether they could cope with it. Most people would know that such an experience must bring shock

99

and grief, but they would probably find it difficult to predict what other emotions they would feel.

Parents of handicapped children do in fact often experience quite complicated and mixed emotions, and sometimes they wonder whether they are very odd in having such emotions. If they do think they are abnormal for feeling as they do, they may hide these emotions from other parents and from the professionals who are helping their child – and so they may never discover that other people feel the same way.

Nobody can take away disturbing emotions altogether; however, it may help to cope with them if you understand them better, especially if you can bring them out into the open and discuss them with other people who have gone through the same experience. This final chapter may make it easier.

But parents of handicapped children are not the only people who have emotions about handicap. The professionals involved with handicapped children are only human. They may have knowledge and experience of a specialist kind (which is what makes them professionals), and this may help them in standing back from the child and being *objective* enough to be useful to him and his family (which is also part of their professionalism). However, they are not *immune* from feelings – in fact, if you meet a professional who really seems to have no natural feelings or emotions, this probably means that he has quite serious emotional hang-ups about whether he is doing his job properly. Some professionals are afraid to show the feelings they have. Sometimes parents of handicapped children find that they not only have to cope with their own emotions, but that they also have to bear an extra stress because of the emotional reactions of one of the professionals who are supposed to be helping them. This ought not to happen, but all too often it does. Here again, it may help to take a cool look at the emotions which professionals may be feeling, because at least this may put things in better perspective.

So what are the emotions which are commonly felt by adults faced with a handicapped child? – and let's remember that nobody is going to have to cope with *all* these emotions at once.

A very experienced paediatrician, Dr Ronald Mac Keith, once made a list of the emotions that parents feel in reaction to handicap, and we don't think we can do better than use his list as a starting point. When we look at professionals' emotions, however, we find that they run surprisingly parallel to those of parents; so we will consider them together.

This is the list:
- Two 'biological' reactions:
    protection of the helpless
    revulsion at the abnormal
- Two feelings of inadequacy:
    inadequacy at reproduction
    inadequacy at rearing

10   Feelings and emotions

- Three feelings of bereavement:
  anger
  grief
  adjustment
- Shock
- Guilt
- Embarrassment

Let's look at these one by one.

'BIOLOGICAL' REACTIONS

Protection of the helpless
By saying this is a 'biological' reaction, Dr MacKeith meant that it is
something deeply built into human nature, and also that it is something that
helps humans to survive. In practice, this means that although almost
everyone would feel extremely alarmed if they were told beforehand that
they would have a severely handicapped child, and might wonder whether
they could possibly be capable of loving and caring for such a child, most
parents do in fact find that, once they actually get to know their child as a
person, they become fiercely protective of him. This feeling leads to the
warm loving care which the child needs from both mother and father (and
mother and father will be able to give much better support *to each other* if
they *both* feel this strong bond to the child – which may not happen if the
parents are separated). In addition, however, the feeling of protection of the
helpless may give the parents strength to fight for their child's rights if these
are not being properly provided. It is a sad fact that necessary provision for
the handicapped can quite often be delayed, or not made available at all, as a
result of cumbersome administrative systems; too much patience is *not* a vir-
tue where getting necessary help for a handicapped child is concerned.

Sometimes parents may find themselves almost being taken over by their
protective feelings, and wanting to protect their child from anything that
might at first bother him. This may be unfair both to the handicapped child
and to his brothers and sisters. There are many reasons why any of us might
become too protective. One is that handicapped children do actually need
more protection than other children, so that we can very easily get into a constant habit of protection, rather than being flexible about it. Another is that
often handicapped children are only too willing to let us do everything for
them because they may not have the urge to independence which normal
children have. Ordinary children literally take things out of our hands; they
refuse to be tied to our apronstrings, because they have a good imagination
that tells them what it might be like to do things for themselves, and a sense
of pride that makes them feel it's good to be independent. Often, with handi-

101

capped children, we have to work hard to make them want independence
and be proud of it.

A third reason has to do with risk-taking. Taking opportunities almost
always means taking risks. Although most of us know that we must let any
child take small risks in order to make progress, with a handicapped child we
are less certain of how well the child will cope with this; and there is also
more real possibility that things could go badly wrong, so that there really is
less margin for error.

> Vincent's mother was regarded by her social worker as 'over-
> protective' because she would not let Vincent, a mentally
> handicapped 12-year-old with some language, go to the corner
> shop on his own. The problem was that nine times out of ten
> Vincent could do this perfectly successfully, but the tenth time
> another child might call out a rude name at him. When that
> happened, Vincent would be extremely upset, and he would not
> have the ordinary social skills just to shout a rude name back, as
> another child would – so he would fling himself to the ground in an
> explosion of misery and frustration, or might just run blindly into the
> distance. Either way, a stranger would have no idea how to deal
> with him.

We can see the problem for Vincent's mother, and it did not help her to be
labelled 'over-protective' – what would have helped much more would have
been to work out a way of allowing Vincent *gradually* to increase the risks.
(She might have tried staying just out of sight, ready to help him deal with
other children, while letting him *think* he was doing it on his own – one family got their neighbours all along the street to peep through the curtains at
their Downs child when she first started shopping expeditions.)

Sometimes parents can rationally accept that their child's growth towards
independence is being stifled by their protectiveness, but still can't bring
themselves to act any differently; or sometimes parents will disagree. If
parents can manage to stay friends about their disagreement and talk it over
between them, then the more protective one may be helped to try out a little
more risk-taking, and their child may benefit enormously. This next mother
had a physically handicapped child; in her case, it was when she married
again that her new husband was able to convince her that her protectiveness
was both acting as a brake on his progress and also making her other children
resentful and jealous.

> 'I'd sort of molly-coddle him, you know, and wrap him in cotton
> wool, and I'd lay there for hours just tickling him while he went to
> sleep, and treating him generally like a baby, you know – I just
> wanted him to myself, I didn't want help from anyone else, or
> anybody else to take him away from me, I just wanted to have him
> as a baby for the rest of his life, really. And it got so bad, I was

102

leaving my other two children out . . . It wasn't until I married Jim that he could point this out to me in a way that I realised what I was doing.'

One other reason why parents feel so protective is that, when your child is having a lot of assessment and treatment in hospitals, it can begin to feel as if he is being taken over by the professionals – as if he has stopped being your child and is becoming just a 'case'. One writer described this feeling in parents as 'the insidious experience of losing control of their child to the medical world'. In a way, having this feeling is a very important attempt to protect the child's *personality* – to remind yourself (and the professionals!) that the child is still a person in his own right. He is not 'a mongol' or 'a Downs', he's not 'a spina bifida', 'an autistic' or 'a microcephalic' – he is, first and foremost, a person, who happens to suffer from problems in these particular categories.

What happens to the feeling of 'protection of the helpless' in professionals?

For many professionals, this is an important reason for having taken up the work they do. They wanted to do something useful with their lives, and giving help where help is needed gives them enormous satisfaction.

Where this can sometimes go wrong is when the feeling of protection leads to professionals taking sides. Children do not usually consult professionals entirely on their own; they come with their parents, and the good professional pays attention to balancing the needs of both child and parent – as well as the needs of other children in the family. Sometimes, though, and especially when these needs clash, he may become so concerned for the child he is treating that he dismisses the parents, or perhaps thinks of them in ways that can very seldom be justified – as over-fussy, over-anxious, unrealistic or unconcerned. One mother, who had been a nurse and now had a deaf and retarded child, said (laughing, but upset as well): 'I knew exactly what was going down in the hospital notes – over-anxious professional mother!'

It is always a great pity when this happens, because it not only makes the professional faulty in his judgement of parents, but also gets in the way of proper communication. In this sort of case, it may sometimes be worthwhile for parents, CALMLY, to ask the professional whether this *is* what he is thinking. At least this will bring it out into the open, and perhaps get communication going between you – there's not much point in just going home to worry about it.

Professionals can also, incidentally, become over-protective of parents; we'll come to this in a minute.

Revulsion at the abnormal

The idea that this is a 'biological' reaction (that is, useful for survi-

103

val) comes from the fact that primitive communities – those who have most difficulty in staying alive anyway – will have still more difficulty if they have to support handicapped members who can't contribute to the hard work of surviving. Some of these communities have therefore encouraged the feeling of revulsion at the abnormal, in order to make it possible for them to drown handicapped babies or leave them to die of exposure. In a civilised society, one of the things that makes us civilised is that we are concerned for the rights and needs of the handicapped person; so that we try to ensure both the child's survival and a reasonable quality of life for him if these are possible.

However, the feeling of revulsion is still a rather deep-seated one, and we need to be aware of that in order not to be too badly upset if we experience it. Many parents of handicapped children will admit that, before they had their own child and got to know him *as a person*, they would turn away from a handicapped child with a feeling of uneasiness, or would feel very uncomfortable in the presence of a retarded adult. Often, parents who feel they have adjusted to their child's handicap, because they now love him for himself, find it extremely disturbing when they first meet a whole group of children with similar handicaps and have to think of their child as belonging to the group. No parents should allow themselves to be *pushed* into this experience; a sensitive group organiser will make it possible for 'new' parents to join such a group as gradually as they wish to.

We've emphasised getting to know a child 'as a person', 'loving him for himself'; and working through feelings of revulsion is very much bound up with how the 'getting-to-know-you' process has happened. There is a big difference between handicaps that gradually appear after parents have had the chance to 'fall in love' with their baby, and those which are obvious at birth so that parents may learn about the handicap even before they've met their baby.

Sometimes things can be made much more difficult for parents by the baby needing immediate treatment which might prevent much contact between parents and child. Nowadays hospitals are much more aware of how important it is for parents to get to know their baby from the start, so that most intensive care units make parents welcome and encourage them to touch and feel and watch their baby, even if they can't hold him yet. At one time it was common to tell a mother 'You've got a spina bifida baby' and then whisk the baby away for treatment in another city, while the mother was left behind to imagine the worst about a baby she had barely seen. It is easier to cope with abnormality if we know what it consists of – and that we have given birth to a living baby, not just to a handicap. Occasionally, however, parents never succeed in finding the baby as a person because they are so totally overwhelmed by their sense of horror at the handicap. Their doctor may possibly share this sense of horror, and therefore be personally unable to help them. If that happens, and parents have given themselves time and still can't change, then it may be better for everyone to accept that the baby might be happier with people who are *not* permanently horrified by him.

Where the baby is mentally very slow, without having any special condition such as Down's syndrome, or where he is spastic or autistic, there will usually be time for his parents to get to know him before they have to think of him as handicapped. This can help the relationship – although it does *not* help if professionals 'protect' the parents by pretending that a child is normal when they know he is not, something which used to happen more than it does now, and which often made parents very bitter and untrusting. Oddly enough, with handicaps that appear late, often the first evidence is the mother's feeling of 'getting the cold shivers' over her baby. It may be quite difficult for her to say exactly what she thinks is the matter, but somehow the baby feels wrong in her arms, or the way he reacts seems vaguely strange to her. Here this slight feeling of revulsion is in fact of use in leading her to get help; and professionals should always take such feelings seriously enough to make a proper investigation.

What about professionals and revulsion?

It is an interesting thought that parents are not supposed to feel revulsion just because they are the parents, whereas professionals are not supposed to feel revulsion because they are professionals. Yet either of them may find themselves with these emotions.

This kind of emotional reaction in the professional can sometimes lead to him apparently dismissing or giving up on a severely handicapped child as though the child no longer existed as a person. Sometimes the way he speaks of the child may show these feelings; professionals have been known to use phrases like 'He's just a vegetable' or 'There's nothing there'. This can be extremely hurtful to parents, who know that there is a *person* there, however little he can do for himself, and who also know that this person is a part of themselves. Parents work through their emotions by keeping the child-as-person in the forefront of their minds; the professional may never work through his because he is continually conscious of the child-as-problem.

Sometimes the professional may feel revulsion for the child combined with protectiveness for the parents; this too can be a difficulty, as it can lead him to give advice which may not be right for this family. Perhaps he feels '*I* couldn't possibly live with this child', and out of misguided sympathy for the parents he may advise 'Put him in a home and forget about him'. Yet the parents may feel quite differently, because they see him as *their* child – not looked-for, yet an important part of how their life has turned out, and certainly not possible to forget about. They may know that one day they might have to think about letting their child go away from home; but they may feel that all they want *now* is some help in keeping him as part of the family. Revulsion in professionals can be dangerous if it first leads them to give 'protective' advice that does not fit the family's needs, and then perhaps prevents them helping in more useful ways when that advice is not accepted.

In all this we have to remember that most parents occasionally feel fed up with their children, handicapped or not, and that these feelings come and go. Parents may have momentary feelings of revulsion and rejection, but overall they may cope perfectly well. The difficulty with professionals' feelings is that they may become 'crystallised' and permanent by being written down in the case-notes. If a hospital professional describes a retarded child as 'this squat pear-shaped little object' in the notes, those are his private feelings talking, and they will not help young nurses who read the notes to see that child as a person. In the same way, if a mother says 'Sometimes I feel as if I couldn't change another nappy' and the professional sympathises so much that he writes this down as 'Care of child causing intolerable stress, residential place urgent', this won't help anyone to make sense of her feelings, which have positives as well as negatives.

A psychologist went to enormous trouble to get a residential place in a psychiatric unit for Simon, a five-year-old autistic child who threw everything in sight. Simon's mother had spent a lot of time telling the psychologist about the throwing and the destruction it caused, because she hoped he would tell her how to deal with it. The psychologist didn't consult her about the unit, because he was afraid he might fail to get a place, and disappoint her; he thought Simon was impossible for an ordinary family to live with. When he told her that he had arranged for Simon to go away, she was horrified and refused to let Simon go. He had expected her to be delighted, and grateful for his efforts; his first feelings when she refused were of anger at his wasted time, rejection and disappointment. This might have ruined their relationship if he had not been able to cope with these emotions, and learn from them.

FEELINGS OF INADEQUACY

Inadequacy at reproduction

What a significant word 'reproduction' is! It underlines the fact that when we have children we expect them to be, at least to some degree, little copies of ourselves. Nobody quite wants an exact copy, of course; but we search in their faces for Mummy's eyes, Daddy's mouth and so on, and we are thrilled and amused if we can detect the family toes on a tiny pink foot.

Most parents have this inner feeling that the child is an advertisement for his parents, and, in a real sense, shows what they are made of. Parents of adopted children often take comfort in blaming the child's heredity if the child doesn't turn out as they hoped. If we give birth to a handicapped child, we may feel deep down that there is something wrong with ourselves because a part of ourselves has turned out imperfect. In most of us there are genes which *could* lead to a handicapped child if various chance factors led that way: and there are many factors which could lead to a child being damaged. The fact that we know 'it might have happened to anybody' doesn't stop us feeling that 'it did happen to us, therefore there must be something wrong with us'.

There seems to be a strong feeling in human beings that they somehow prove themselves as whole people by reproducing themselves. People who cannot have children often feel 'not properly whole'; people who *choose* not to have children often find that others regard them with pity or disgust, and may see them as 'unfulfilled' or 'selfish'. We can't help seeing ourselves as others see us, in the sense that, if society behaves as if we can only prove ourselves by having a perfect child, we soon begin to feel as if this were true.

These feelings can unfortunately strike deep at a parent's self-confidence, just at a time when parents need all the confidence they can get. Sometimes only one parent is affected by these emotions: more often fathers, perhaps because men's pride seems more easily hurt. One of the parents may, out of this feeling of hurt, turn against the other in order to lay the blame somewhere: 'It didn't come from *my* side of the family!' – and sometimes grandparents, sadly, can encourage this. It is a very understanding wife or husband who can recognise these hurt feelings for what they are, and not become angry in turn.

Brothers and sisters may also suffer from similar feelings: 'If my brother is like this', they may wonder, 'might there not be something wrong with me too, perhaps inside where it doesn't show *yet*?' Other children can cruelly back up such feelings by teasing them or talking as if the handicap were 'catching'. The normal twin of a handicapped child can feel particularly confused, since most people tend to think of twins as a closely identified pair. Feelings of uncertainty like this can lead to apparent 'naughtiness' in a brother or sister, which is really a way of drawing parents' attention to their unhappiness. It can help a lot if parents show that they understand these feelings and have themselves experienced them.

Inadequacy at rearing

Parents of handicapped children have every opportunity to prove themselves as whole people by coping with the enormous demands that are made on them in rearing a child with special needs; in fact, some come to feel that the experience of becoming a whole person is what a handicapped child gives his parents. 'I didn't know I was born before we had him,' said the father of an autistic child. 'I didn't know what families were for, I didn't know what a friend was. It's taught me about the meaning of things, and that can't be bad.'

But it takes time to come to such a viewpoint. We are seldom given time to prepare ourselves for being the parent of a handicapped baby. Although most young parents are fairly inexperienced when they have their first child, at least they can see around them the evidence that mothers and fathers fairly quickly get the hang of looking after babies. We are much less likely to see around us how to bring up a handicapped child; all we know is that it must be much more difficult. So most parents, faced with a handicapped child, will at some time have felt very panicky about the question 'Will I do it wrong?' On top of that, there's the question 'Am I a strong enough personality to cope?' Bringing up a handicapped child is not just a job, it's a personal commitment – and none of us know whether we are capable of it until we are made to try.

Panic about feelings of inadequacy in rearing can occasionally cause a parent literally to run away – to reject the child – and this is one reason why there needs to be capable, constructive and *realistic* help available both early on and later from professionals. Professionals may not fully enter into parents' feelings, if they have not experienced them as parents themselves, but at least they have knowledge which parents can use. YOU MUST ASK QUESTIONS, because some professionals believe that no questions *asked* means that none *exist*.

For some parents, 'Will I do it wrong?' is not the only anxiety; they may for a long time be haunted by the question '*Did* I do it wrong?' This is particularly true of autistic children's parents, where the child at first seems quite normal, but where his behaviour gradually becomes more and more difficult to understand. Although the autism was there all along, it does not show clearly as a handicap until we begin to make bigger demands on the child than we did when he was tiny – and because the child *looks* normal, at first he may just seem unusually naughty, or miserable, or unable to respond to us. No wonder autistic children's parents ask themselves whether they are doing it wrong – what they could possibly have done to make the child like this. Autism is perhaps the most bewildering of all handicaps, and is also much more rare than most handicaps – which is why these parents especially need to find someone quickly who can help them make sense of their child.

Professional feelings of inadequacy
Professionals tend to feel inadequate in rather different ways, but they still have these feelings. Some feelings of inadequacy they have to learn to live with, because the feelings are a part of the situation. For instance, doctors usually have in the backs of their minds the need to cure people – but most handicaps cannot be cured, only alleviated, and this may make them feel inadequate as doctors. Some professionals feel inadequate because they are so aware of the burdens suffered by parents, yet cannot shoulder those burdens themselves – and this feeling too is something they must

learn to accept, though it may help to make them more caring and helpful. There are other feelings which have more to do with their doubts about their competence. Anyone doing a job may sometimes wonder whether they have done it as well as they could. These doubts are useful, for they make us criticise ourselves and learn to do better. However, the doubts that can arise for a professional working with handicapped children and their families may cause more emotion and more uncertainty because more is at stake: it matters a great deal that he should do his job properly.

When people feel uncertain about how well they are doing their job, sometimes they react by defending themselves against criticism. It takes confidence to accept criticism gracefully and learn by it, or to admit that other professionals might not agree with your judgement. One way in which this can arise is where parents ask for a second opinion. A confident professional will accept such a request, recognising that parents need to be sure about the needs of their child; he will help them to find a second opinion, and assure them that he will still be available for consultation afterwards. The defensive professional may feel very threatened by such a request, and may even show this by asking needlessly aggressive questions, such as 'Are you doubting my professional competence?' He may give parents the impression that he will resist or oppose their wish for a second opinion, and may suggest that he will abandon the case if they persist. It is very difficult for parents to remain calm and reasonable in such a situation; it may help to realise that the professional is putting on a cloak of authority to hide his uncertainty about himself. Remind yourself that when professionals themselves have a handicapped child, they are even more likely than other parents to look for a second opinion. Dr. Mac Keith, writing for his follow-doctors, said:

'A doctor who feels he is reasonably competent, and who has given adequate attention and time to the parents, may regret that he has failed to meet their needs, but he will understand why they feel they must ask for a further opinion.'

Some professionals feel inadequate at communicating well with parents; as a result, they may speak to parents gruffly or impersonally, perhaps almost seeming embarrassed. Parents may then feel the professional is embarrassed about the child, or about them; he is more likely to be embarrassed over his own inadequacy. Some, because they are not good at communicating, leave a junior colleague to break unhappy news or explain what the handicap means; they are wrong to do this, because such explanations are their responsibility if they are in charge of the case, but again it is something which can stem from their feelings of inadequacy.

One other way in which professionals can show a lack of real confidence is to put up defences of various sorts which save them having to explain themselves fully to parents. They may use 'jargon' in a defensive way, using a technical term and not offering to explain it, so that they need not go into what it implies. They may be unwilling to admit that they simply do not, and perhaps cannot, know the answers to certain questions. They may hide behind the barrier of a secretary in order not to have to face parents; or they may entrench themselves behind large desks, and fail to look up from their notes when parents enter the room. In all this, they are relying on parents being too polite to insist on straight answers; as one paediatrician remarked, 'Too often parents try to save their doctor distress'.

The difficulty of being a 'professionalised' parent

There is another problem of 'feeling inadequate' which perhaps we should discuss at this point. It arises out of the need for parents to learn special skills in order to help their handicapped child. Parents of children who are physically disabled learn to measure drugs, carry out physiotherapy and become skilled nurses; parents of children with sensory or mental handicaps often have to learn (some from handbooks like this!) skilled ways of 'getting through' to the child.

The difficulty is that most parents like to feel that being a parent is something that comes naturally. Although most parents do deliberately teach any child from time to time (hearing them read, helping with sums and so on), using *professional skills* to help a child learn doesn't quite feel the same as just being a mum or being a dad – perhaps because most of us grow up expecting to be parents, whereas few of us expect to be teachers or therapists.

But being mum or dad to a handicapped child suddenly shows that we need these special skills if we are to do our best for him. It's something we can learn and cope with if we have to. Given the opportunity, parents mostly manage it very well. Just as most of us, without much experience, can cope with becoming a parent, so we can also learn the role of professionally skilled parent.

A more difficult thing, though, is balancing the roles of 'professional parent' to the handicapped child and 'ordinary parent' to the other children in the family, both at the same time. Many parents find this continual switching very stressful indeed. Some cope with it by confiding in the other children and letting them help a bit with the teaching programme; many brothers and sisters are extraordinarily good at this, so long as it is not allowed to become a burden. Where the other children are very young, this is not so easy. In this case it can be particularly helpful if father and mother can each give each other time off from the handicapped child, in which to enjoy the other children in a relaxed way; or single parents may be able to work out a baby-sitting rota with a friend. Every parent of both a normal and a handicapped child should have a time for single-mindedly giving attention to one child at a time; and every normal child needs that opportunity too. This could be a worthwhile project for a local voluntary society.

110

FEELINGS OF BEREAVEMENT: GRIEF, ANGER AND ADJUSTMENT

The feelings of grief and anger, and the experience of adjustment, are all normal parts of bereavement; but why should we think of the diagnosis of a handicapped child as a bereavement, when the child is still there?

To understand this, we have to remember that no child is completely new to its mother at birth. She has been carrying him inside her, and thinking about him, for the past nine months; in a sense, she has made friends with the baby *as she thinks he is*. She has imagined what he will be like; not just as a baby, but what it will be like to have a growing-up child. Research has been done in which mothers were asked to describe the personality of their one-day-old child, and it was found that they had a very complete idea of what they thought he might be like. It is this *imagined* child who has been lost when a handicapped child is born; so that grief for a lost child is added to grief for the problems of the child who exists.

With a handicapped child who is diagnosed some time after his birth, or who develops a handicap, the bereavement is slightly different but just as great, and for the father it may be greater. Here the parents have not just their imagined baby to grieve for, but the child who had already taken his place in the family and whom they believed to be normal. Parents don't necessarily have firm plans for their children; but they do often have dreams and fancies, which are dealt a death-blow by the diagnosis of handicap. One mother said of her mildly brain-damaged son: 'He'll never make the school football team, will he?' That was the least of her worries, and yet it expressed all the shattered fantasies that go to make up the hurt of bereavement.

Grief is the most expected emotion in bereavement, but anger is almost as common. Its most usual form is the feeling of 'Why pick on us?' – an anger against fate, for being so unfair. We unconsciously expect life to be fair, and also to have some warning before a disaster. When what seems to be a total disaster comes at us out of the blue, the feeling 'We didn't deserve this' can lead to overwhelming anger.

Parents often also feel as if a bargain has been broken. In settling down and having a family, most of us are making a silent agreement that we are now committing ourselves to being responsible parents – the longest-term commitment that we have ever taken on. With a handicapped child, suddenly we find that we have taken on a quite different bargain: overnight the terms of the agreement have been changed, from the twenty-year contract we accepted, to what now looks as if it might be a life sentence – and nobody consulted us first. No wonder some parents feel battered and violated – that 'things were never meant to be like this', that 'this wasn't the package deal I bargained for'. Sometimes special circumstances will make parents feel still more bitter and cheated. A father whose wife had had difficulty in conceiving in the first place still could not adjust to life's unfairness years after his mentally handicapped daughter was born, despite his love and care for the child: 'We waited for her ten years', he said, 'and this is what we get!'

Most people, when they are angry, feel better when they have expressed their feelings. The trouble is that when you are angry with 'life' or 'fate', there's no-one there to be angry *with*. Some parents lose their religious faith at this point – in short, they express their anger against God. Others have no faith to lose: or, the opposite, find that a belief in God gives them a sense of purpose – a role in caring for the helpless – which is lacking from the idea of a cruel unpredictable fate.

People who are angry against someone or something that they can't get at may often express their anger against whoever is at hand, often someone who may not deserve it at all. Someone who is told off by his boss may come home and kick the cat, shout at the children and pick a quarrel with his wife; in the same way, parents who feel angry at fate may start picking on each other, or on their other children, in ways which they cannot afford to do if they want to gain strength from each other.

Looking after the child may exhaust one of the parents and make the other resentful that the pleasant companionship they once enjoyed seems to have been sacrificed to the child's needs. At the same time, bottling up anger can itself cause cracks in a marriage; parents may need to admit to each other just how much resentment and misery they have been feeling, in order to take another look at their situation and see how it might be eased, even in small ways.

Sometimes parents will take out their anger on the nearest professional – who, because he does happen to be around, may well also be their most supportive professional. Obviously, venting your anger against fate on the professional who is supporting you is a bit risky. Professionals are human, and to be met with anger when they thought they were doing their best can arouse their resentment and an angry response. The good professional, though, will understand where the anger came from and what it meant, and can accept and 'absorb' it without bearing a grudge.

However, not all anger comes out of grief. Sometimes parents want to express rational anger because they feel critical of what has been done – or not done. For this reason if for no other, it may be helpful to recognise in yourself the emotional, cursing-fate kind of anger, and to be prepared to explain to the professional that this was what it was about when you were going on at him. Then when you really do feel critical, you will be able to say 'but this time I'm *reasonably* angry'.

The feelings of grief and anger can take a very long time to work through, and adjustment to such a changed situation is usually very gradual indeed.

Sometimes people almost resist adjustment; there is the feeling that to get to the point where this new kind of life seemed normal would almost be a disaster in itself. This is similar to the feelings of a bereaved wife or husband: that to begin to feel happy again is a kind of betrayal.

Yet human beings are amazingly capable of adjustment, and this is their strength. The most surprising thing about living with a severely handicapped child, which from the outside looks intolerable, is that families do manage to describe themselves as 'happy'. These families have learned to live with what various people have described as 'chronic sorrow', 'a sense of continuing pain', 'an interminable crisis' – and yet have found the blessings, the positive things, the satisfactions, which have made them feel it was bearable, worthwhile or even enriching of their lives; though rather few would *choose* a handicapped child, if they could start again.

People who have been widowed often say that the worst part is not at the beginning, when you are getting sympathy and support in the crisis; it is two, three or more years on, when you are supposed to have got used to the idea and made the adjustment. The same is often true for parents of a handicapped child. Partly this goes back to our parental dreams. It may be that what a particular parent most looked forward to in motherhood or fatherhood was not the baby stage at all, but sharing interests with a seven-year-old or having a grown-up son or daughter to be companionable with. Parents of teenaged handicapped children, who thought that they had adjusted well to the situation, can suddenly find themselves feeling deeply depressed or grief-stricken, as they see around them independent young people doing all the things that sum up what their child can never be. However much they love him, this can hit very hard – especially if they have no other children, or if their other children are of a different sex. If their only 'grown-up son' or 'grown-up daughter' is in fact permanently a child, it is at this stage that their grief may sharply return – and at this stage the support services for parents may be difficult to find.

In recent years there have been increasing attempts to help parents take an active and constructive part in working remedially with their child. This book is one of them. Sometimes professionals, in their eagerness to get things going for the child, may push parents too hard and too quickly. It also has to be admitted that some professionals are very much afraid of grief, especially if they themselves have not experienced it in their own lives. Knowing that it can help a grieving person to have positive things to do, the professional in his enthusiasm may almost seem to deny that the grief exists. This positive approach does help some parents; but others may want to face their grief first and work their way through it gradually. If you feel pressured by too much 'positiveness', don't be afraid to say 'Stop – give me time. Let me find my way at my own pace'. You might be speaking for others beside yourself.

113

FEELINGS OF SHOCK

In some ways, shock is another of the feelings of bereavement – or at least, it has a good deal in common with the feelings of numbness and disbelief which bereaved people experience. Parents describe themselves as 'feeling I was trapped in a bad dream', 'hearing this great bell in my head going *spastic – spastic – spastic*', 'feeling I just didn't want to wake up to another day'.

A Downs baby's father describes it like this:

> 'When you are told that your child is abnormal in some way, you are assailed by the most extraordinary feeling of bleakness and complete despair. When it happened to me, I felt sort of detached and outside myself in a way I have not experienced before or since. There is the feeling that the world and all the people in it have changed, and that things will never be the same again. There is a sense of complete isolation and of difference. You find yourself grappling with feelings which you don't understand, and with thoughts which are so dreadful that you dare not mention them to anyone.'

When we are in a state of shock, it is difficult to take in what is said to us; and what we do take in, we may not trust, because our senses don't feel as if they're working properly. Also, the reason we are in a state of shock is that the news is worse than we ever expected. For these reasons, one of the results of shock is likely to be disbelief: in a sense, we defend ourselves against the coming grief by telling ourselves that this can't possibly have happened. This feeling of disbelief can last for a very long time, and its final disappearance can itself be a shock.

> Jilly's parents were both professionals themselves. They had been told that Jilly was spastic when she was 15 months old. They apparently accepted this, and offered that Jilly's physical problems should be demonstrated to students in their own department by a specialist from a famous centre, which was done when she was 19 months old. Halfway through the demonstration, Jilly's mother was clearly in a state of shock. It was only then that she realised that she had been hoping against hope that the specialist would say Jilly was normal after all; it was the specialist's matter-of-fact *assumption* that Jilly was spastic that forced her to face this truth head-on.

Parents sometimes complain that their child's condition has never been properly explained to them, while their professional advisers protest that they *have* explained in great detail when the diagnosis was given. This disagreement comes from the professional not having realised how overwhelming the shock could be; the parents may hardly have heard his explanation because of the frightening words clanging away in their minds, and certainly they will have had difficulty taking it in and remembering it in detail. This is one reason why it is important for professionals both to write down a full explanation for parents (parents should ask for this if it is not offered), and to make sure that parents have a later appointment to discuss all they want to know when they feel better able to listen properly.

FEELINGS OF GUILT

Some professionals have thought in the past that all parents of handicapped children suffer from a sense of guilt at bringing a handicapped baby into the world. This is not true; and the belief has caused a good deal of irritation to parents who have been advised that they must not feel guilty, when in fact they are feeling nothing of the kind.

What we have to remember is that parents – any parents – very easily do feel guilty when things go wrong for their children. Parents generally know that bringing up children is the biggest responsibility they will ever have; so it is natural for them to ask themselves 'Is it my fault?' when normal children are over-shy, or bad-tempered, or tell lies, or get too fat. A handicapped child just makes parents more likely to feel normal parental guilt.

However, there are also other reasons why parents might feel over-guilty if their child is handicapped. One is that deep down in most people's beliefs is the idea that you get what you deserve – a kind of magical idea, left over from primitive times. We've already mentioned the 'why me?' feeling which makes people angry that they have got something they *didn't* deserve. This also works the other way round; we may feel that disaster must be a punishment for *something*, and this may make us feel guilty even though we don't know what we're being punished for. Very few people are perfect, so there's usually room for us to feel guilty anyway, even if only for thinking unkind thoughts!

Another quite important reason why parents might begin to feel guilty is that society tends to treat parents of handicapped children almost as if they *were* guilty. Suddenly the family's life is opened up to be inspected. You have to keep taking your child to be looked at and tested; you are asked all sorts of intimate questions; you have to accept people coming into your house, whom you do not necessarily know; you are told how to behave with your child; judgements are made and decisions are taken, not always consulting you in much detail. Of course, it's all intended for the good of the child; but it's not surprising that parents often feel as if they're at least on probation, if not on trial.

Many parents also feel guilty because, in doing their best for a child who has such enormous needs, they know that their other children are losing out. That kind of guilt can be an important reminder; sometimes parents do need to reconsider whether the balance of their attention, tipped as it may

115

have to be towards the weakest child, might have tipped too far. Parents have to decide this one for themselves; but they could do worse than ask the other children what *they* think about it. Children can be amazingly mature and understanding if they are given the opportunity of an honest discussion, rather than being left to nurse their resentment.

Professionals, too, can suffer from feelings of guilt, and perhaps this is especially true for the medical profession. We've already pointed out that doctors are trained to cure people, and may feel very inadequate when they cannot. They are also trained to *prevent* disease and damage; and in that sense, every handicapped child seems like a medical failure, reminding doctors that there are still many problems that they have not yet solved.

An even more bitter thought is that there are some handicaps which may actually have been caused by what seemed to be medical progress. An obvious example is the thalidomide tragedy; another is 'vaccine damage', although this is difficult to prove. Doctors have to accept professional responsibility for such possibilities, even if not personal responsibility; and this may certainly give rise to personal feelings of guilt.

Although some family doctors are enormously supportive to parents with handicapped children, dropping in regularly to make sure things are going reasonably well, others surprise and hurt parents by ignoring the existence of the handicapped child, as if they had never heard the term 'family doctor'. In some cases, this may be because the doctor feels this is no longer his job, having passed on the child to the specialist; but very often there is strong evidence for thinking that the child makes the doctor feel guilty and inadequate, and is ignored for that reason. This can also happen with other professionals; a psychologist or a therapist may find a child particularly difficult to work with, and this may cause them to feel guilty about their own lack of skill – their visits may actually stop as a result. At this point it may be that the parents have to support the professional, by showing that they understand how difficult it is but *still* want the professional to try and help!

FEELINGS OF EMBARRASSMENT

Embarrassment doesn't seem a very important emotion, compared with all the big emotions that we've talked about; but many parents find it very troubling, and one of the most difficult to deal with at first.

Embarrassment is what we feel when we don't know quite how to behave in a certain situation, and when we are worried about what other people are thinking. It's a word that keeps cropping up when parents of handicapped children are talking about their daily lives, especially the early days.

Early on, parents are embarrassed because there is no set way of announcing that your baby is handicapped. If the baby is known to be handicapped from birth, parents have to cope with the congratulations of their neighbours, and then watch their faces change as they learn the news. At that point it is the neighbours who are embarrassed; faced with this grief, what can they say? Some people instinctively say or do the right thing, and then both can be at ease with no more embarrassment; others are frightened off by their own inability to express themselves. Parents often say that their suffering is doubled by finding that some neighbours avoid them, even crossing the street so as not to have to comment on the baby.

This is one reason why the various voluntary groups and societies can be so helpful to parents: there need be no embarrassment because all the members know what it is to find oneself with a handicapped child. Much of the sympathy does not even need to be spoken; it can be taken for granted, along with the practical hints and ideas that are exchanged. However, here again some parents will not want to be pressed to join such a group before they feel ready. To join this kind of group is to accept being identified as, in a sense, a 'handicapped parent'. However great the benefits, this is not what everybody wants when they are still trying to get used to handicap as an idea.

Later in the child's life, the embarrassment may come from what he does rather than how people react to what he is. Children who scream or make other odd noises; children who sniff at other customers in the supermarket, or go through their handbags in the queue at the checkout; children who look normal but won't say a word – or only say swear-words; children who run endlessly, or throw whatever they can pick up: all these children make it difficult for parents to behave normally in public places. One mother said 'I deeply resent the fact that I have had to become an apologetic person'. Here again, sharing such experiences with other parents can help in growing a thick skin and a sense of humour to protect you from people who do not understand; for the hard truth is that parents who don't manage this can become very isolated and cut off by their fear of going out.

Carrying out some of the ideas in this book (and in other such books) may lead to embarrassment; the best thing for the child may not be what the public expects. Tracey's parents (page 16), sitting in the café trying to ignore her swearing, are a good example. Here are two more:

> Janie, whose appearance was normal, at 12 was very frightened of lifts. Her mother regularly took her in lifts, however, keeping her calm by stroking her hair and repeating 'Good girl, Janie. You *are* a brave girl. Well done!' and so on. She got some very strange looks, but Janie's fear decreased.

> Luke's foster-mother was trying to teach him to wait his turn patiently. Frustrated at a check-out, he said loudly 'I'd like to kick that man!' His foster-mother replied calmly, 'I know you would, but you're not going to'. Her acceptance of his wishes, while assuring him that he *would* control himself, was helpful in actually

teaching him control; but again, she had to put up with shocked looks from people who thought she should have smacked him, or at least been angry.

Professionals, too, can be embarrassed: rarely at what a child might say or do, but sometimes at their own difficulty in expressing themselves sensitively. As we mentioned earlier, parents can sometimes misinterpret this, and think that the professional finds their child embarrassing. Occasionally parents of a child already known to be physically handicapped feel that they cannot get the professional in charge of the case to discuss the possibility of mental handicap, and are hurt by the feeling that their wish to do so embarrasses him. If this is so, it is probably his own sense of inadequacy which is at fault, and perhaps, again, a fear of parents' grief. Parents may need to assure the professional that they really do want to know the answers to these questions, and perhaps should ask for another opinion if they really cannot get an answer that they are satisfied is frank and open.

FINALLY:

Parents and professionals are faced with very different problems when they try to do their best for a handicapped child. For a start, professionals go off duty, which parents seldom do. Secondly, professionals' emotions are usually about *themselves as professionals*; whereas parents' emotions are about *themselves as parents* – a much more basic and long-term role. Professionals who have handicapped children of their own tend to find that their ability to cope with this has more to do with the kind of people they are, than the kind of professional training they have: that is, faced with a handicapped child in their own family, their parenthood is more important than their professionalism.

From the child's point of view, parents have big advantages because they are emotionally committed to him and because they know him as a person so well. The advantages that professionals have are the skills and knowledge that come from their training, and the perspective that comes from experience of many handicapped children. When professionals share these advantages with parents, parents undoubtedly become the most effective members of the team that is working for the child.

Brothers and sisters have also come up a number of times in this chapter. It is hardly possible for the situation not to be stressful for them, though they may eventually become stronger people through these experiences. If they are fortunate, they will feel they have a secure place both as part of the family and as part of the team; remembering always that they are family members first and foremost. Often brothers and sisters may feel that the handicapped child causes them problems which they are unwilling to mention to their parents – children can be very protective of parents' feelings! Some special schools have recognised this need by organising conferences and discussion groups in which the brothers and sisters can share their feelings and discover that they are not alone. Parents who ask their local society or school to organise such a meeting may be showing their own understanding in a particularly valuable way.

We are convinced that parents – and other family members – must be recognised as central figures in the lives of children, and that professionals must be willing to *share* their knowledge and understanding if a true and worthwhile partnership is to be built up. We want to see this become a reality for all parents of handicapped children; and that, in a nutshell, is why we have written this book.

Appendix 1   **Developmental checklist**

We are grateful to Phil Christie for allowing us to use a very much shortened form of a checklist devised by him.

Ages are given in years and months, i.e. 1:3 means 1 year and 3 months. *These ages are all approximate and not exact.*

A. LARGE BODY MOVEMENTS

		Age expected
1	When held sitting will hold head steady for several seconds	0:3
2	When lying on back will raise arms to grasp dangling object	0:6
3	Can roll from tummy to back	0:6
4	When held in standing position will bear own weight	0:6
5	Will sit unsupported for several minutes	0:9
6	When held standing will step on alternate feet	0:9
7	Walks with one hand held	1:0
8	Will stand unsupported for a few moments	1:0
9	Can walk alone with unsteady steps	1:3
10	Can crawl upstairs	1:3
11	Can push large wheeled toys	1:6
12	Will walk upstairs (two feet per step) holding on to rail/wall	2:0
13	Can kick ball gently	2:0
14	Can jump from low step with two feet together	2:6
15	Can sit on and steer tricycle, scooting with feet on floor	2:6
16	Can catch large ball on or between extended arms	3:0
17	Is able to walk upstairs, one foot per step	3:0
18	Can balance, for a moment, on one foot	3:0
19	Can walk downstairs, one foot per step	4:0
20	Is able to pedal tricycle without help	4:0

120

Appendix 1   Developmental checklist

B. HAND–EYE CO-ORDINATION

		Age expected
1	Will grasp and shake rattle when placed in hand	0:4
2	Can pass toy from one hand to another	0:6
3	Can hold cube in each hand without dropping either	0:7
4	Can pick up small object (e.g. Smartie) between thumb and rest of hand	0:9
5	Can pick up Smartie between thumb and forefinger only	1:0
6	Will scribble spontaneously	1:6
7	Is able to imitate building of three-cube tower	1:9
8	Can unwrap a small sweet	2:0
9	Can copy drawing of vertical line	2:0
10	Will make train of bricks (four or more cubes)	2:0
11	Can turn door knob	2:0
12	Is able to copy drawings of horizontal line and circle	2:6
13	Will thread large beads on to shoe lace	3:0
14	Imitates building bridge out of three cubes	3:0
15	Shows mature pencil grasp	4:0
16	Can draw figure with head, legs and sometimes trunk	4:6
17	Can cut along straight line with scissors	4:6

C. COMMUNICATION

1	Is quietened by voice of adult	0:1
2	Will make vocalisation other than crying	0:2
3	Will make some vocalisation when spoken to	0:3
4	Raises arms to be picked up	0:6
5	Will turn to mother's voice across room	0:6
6	Will vocalise to attract attention	0:9
7	Demonstrates understanding of 'no'	0:9
8	Can imitate sounds made by adults (e.g. cough)	0:9
9	Waves goodbye	0:9
10	Responds to own name	0:10
11	Can imitate simple actions (e.g. hand-clapping)	1:0
12	Can imitate long vowel sounds (e.g. 'ah', 'oh', 'ee')	1:0
13	Shows understanding of simple instructions used with gesture (e.g. 'give it to mummy')	1:0
14	Will point with forefinger at objects which are out of reach	1:0
15	Can use several words singly in correct context	1:3
16	Will hand familiar objects to adults when asked for by name	1:6
17	Indicates wanted objects by naming	1:6
18	Has around 20+ clear words	2:0

121

Appetite Appendix 1   Developmental checklist

Age expected

19	Can form simple sentences with two or more words	2:0
20	Refers to self by name	2:0
21	Can use 'I', 'me', 'you', correctly	2:6
22	Asks questions using 'who', 'what', 'where'	2:6

D. PLAY

1	Follows moving person with eyes	0:2
2	Increases activity at sight of interesting object	0:4
3	Fingers own reflection in mirror	0:6
4	Plays peep-bo	0:9
5	Looks for toy which has been dropped	0:9
6	Can find a hidden toy (e.g. under a cup)	1:0
7	Rattles spoon in cup, or bangs two spoons together, in imitation	1:0
8	Will put wooden cube in and out of box	1:0
9	Actively explores objects and will repeat activities with a sound-making toy	1:3
10	Remembers where familiar objects are kept	1:3
11	Briefly imitates 'tool' action (e.g. brushing teeth, sweeping floor)	1:6
12	Will put as many as ten wooden cubes into a box	1:6
13	Engages in simple make-believe play	2:0
14	Will play near other children but not join in	2:0
15	Watches other children play and joins in briefly	2:6
16	Enjoys painting – will make dots, lines and circular shapes	3:0
17	Will match two or three colours	3:0
18	Actively joins in play with other children	3:0

E. FEEDING

1	Will feed from spoon	0:3
2	Can hold biscuit and take to mouth	0:6
3	Will drink from bottle held by self	0:9
4	Can drink from cup with help	1:0
5	Uses fingers for eating	1:0
6	Can hold spoon but not take food to mouth	1:0
7	Holds spoon, takes to mouth but turns over	1:3
8	Holds spoon and takes food safely to mouth	1:6
9	Chews well	1:6
10	Drinks from cup unaided (some spilling)	1:6
11	Spoon-feeds unaided (some spilling)	2:0
12	Can raise cup to drink and replace on table	2:0

122

Appendix 1   Developmental checklist

		Age expected
13	Can use fork/spoon appropriately	3:0
14	Pours from jug to cup and stops before liquid reaches top	3:0
15	Can use knife and fork together	4:6
16	Can use knife for spreading	6:0

F. DRESSING

1	Can take loose covering from head	0:4
2	Will hold out arms for sleeves	1:0
3	Will hold out foot for shoe	1:0
4	Will struggle into/out of vest if half over head	1:3
5	Can use feet to push off shoes when sitting	1:3
6	Can take off shoes with hands	1:6
7	Can take off socks	1:9
8	Can take off unbuttoned coat	1:9
9	Can completely remove pants	2:0
10	Is able to unzip garment	2:0
11	Can find armholes when putting on coat	2:6
12	Is able to remove all clothes already unfastened	2:9
13	Can put on simple articles (e.g. pants, socks) (not always right way round)	3:0
14	Can undo large buttons	3:0
15	Can untie laces	3:0
16	Distinguishes front and back of garment	4:0
17	Can do up easy buttons	4:0
18	Can dress and undress completely except back buttons and laces	4:6
19	Can dress and undress without assistance (not always laces)	5:0

123

Appendix 2 **Book list**

There are hundreds of books on handicap. These are the ones which we think are especially helpful. A longer list can be obtained on request from the Child Development Research Unit, Nottingham University – please send a postage stamp.

1. BOOKS TO TAKE YOU FURTHER IN WORKING AND CARING FOR YOUR CHILD

Helping your Handicapped Baby by Chris Cunningham and Patricia Sloper, Souvenir Press, 1978.

Let me Play and *Teaching the Handicapped Child*, both by Dorothy Jeffree, Roy McConkey and Simon Hewson, Souvenir Press, 1977.

Let me Speak by Dorothy Jeffree and Roy McConkey, Souvenir Press, 1976.
    These four are all based on highly practical research with mentally handicapped children, and suggest many well-tried ideas, including designs for special toys and how to use them.

The First Words Language Programme and *Two Words Together* by Bill Gillham, Allen and Unwin, 1979 and 1982. Practical programmes for teaching first a useful vocabulary, then early sentence-making.

Encouraging Language Development by Phyllis Hastings and Bessie Hayes, Croom Helm, 1981. Follows on from *Two Words Together* – Bill Gillham co-ordinates this series.

Toys and Playthings in Development and Remediation by John and Elizabeth Newson, Penguin Books, 1979. Looks at toys and how they focus and sustain play in both normal and handicapped children; especially useful for parents who have both, as it relates slow development to normal development.

Toys and Play for the Handicapped Child by Barbara Riddick, Croom Helm, 1982. By a child psychologist experienced in toy library work with pre-school children.

124

ABC of Toys, Toy Libraries Association (see 'useful addresses'). A 'good toy' guide, written with the special needs of handicapped children in mind and updated every year. Also write to TLA for their list of booklets.

A Source Book for the Disabled, edited by Glorya Hale, Imprint Books, 1979. Ideas for helping the physically disabled to manage more independently, with a good chapter on the disabled child: shows special aids.

Your Child is Different, edited by David Mitchell, published by Radio New Zealand, 1979. If you can get it, this is an excellent book, both thoughtful and practical, and written in simple friendly language.

Helping Your Handicapped Child, by Janet Carr, Penguin, 1980. Behavioural approach, lots of detail on keeping records etc.

Starting Off by Chris Kiernan, Rita Jordan and Chris Saunders, Souvenir Press, 1978. Takes the behavioural ideas in this book further; also has very informative chapters on signing systems and physiotherapy approaches.

A Step-by-Step Learning Guide for Retarded Infants and Children and *A Step-by-Step Learning Guide for Older Retarded Children*, both by Vicky Johnson and Roberta Werner, Constable, 1980. Recipe-book approach, and a very good one as such. Each contains well over 200 recipes (they call them 'tasks', but don't be put off!) for ways of teaching your child.

In Search of a Curriculum by the staff of Rectory Paddock School, Robin Wren Publications (ISBN 0 9507759 0 8), 1981. Written by teachers for teachers about the education of severely handicapped children; quite difficult specialist language, but worth the effort.

Understanding the Deaf–Blind Child by Peggy Freeman, Heinemann, 1974. Many good ideas for 'getting through' to any cut-off child, not just this very difficult group; written from a parent's experience.

Handling the Young Cerebral Palsied Child at Home by Nancie Finnie, Heinemann, 1974. Written by an outstanding physiotherapist out of her commitment to parents as well as children, and helpfully illustrated.

Autistic Children: a guide for parents by Lorna Wing, Constable, 1980. Written by a psychiatrist specialising in autism who is also the mother of an autistic child; especially useful on the more severely handicapped child.

2. BOOKS IN WHICH PARENTS SHARE THEIR
EXPERIENCES OF HANDICAP, OR WHICH QUOTE
PARENTS IN DETAIL

The Family and the Handicapped Child by Sheila Hewett, Allen and Unwin, 1970. Study of 180 families containing a cerebral palsied child.

The Deaf Child and his Family by Susan Gregory, Allen and Unwin, 1976. Similar study, 122 families.

Parents and Children in Autism by Marian de Myer, Wiley, 1979. Looks at the different problems that arise for parents, mainly through their eyes.

Parents and Mentally Handicapped Children by Charles Hannam, Penguin
Books, 1980. Interviews with parents of eight mentally handicapped children. The author has a Downs (mongol) child.

A Mentally Handicapped Child in the Family by Mary McCormack, Constable, London, 1978. Looks at most of the problems that concern parents
with extensive illustration from individual case histories and parents' discussion; the writer has a brain-damaged child.

A Difference in the Family by Helen Featherstone, Basic Books, 1980. The
American educationalist mother of a severely multi-handicapped child
focuses particularly on the emotions generated in and between family
members. There are sensitive discussions of marital stress and of the
brothers and sisters; and an excellent reference list of other parents'
accounts of their own individual experiences, for further reading.

3. BOOKS FOR YOUR HANDICAPPED CHILD

Picture books with simple clear pictures to name and talk about are not
always easy to find. Photographs tend to be best to start with, as they are
more realistic.

The First Words Picture Book by Bill Gillham, Methuen, 1982. Dr Gillham
(see earlier) is a psychologist who has specialised in encouraging speech in
slow-learning children; clear photographs of a familiar object on one
page, with the same object shown in use opposite, therefore ideal for
'naming and talking about'.

Look and See Books, Methuen, 1980. Series of eight photographic card
books on a similar principle, focused on everyday activities like Bathtime,
Mealtime and so on.

Baby Board Books by Helen Oxenbury, Methuen, 1981. Series of five on
similar principles, using drawings, therefore slightly more difficult.

This Little Puffin by E. Matterson, Penguin Books, 1969. A treasury of new
and old lap rhymes and finger play.

Finger Rhymes, *Action Rhymes* and *Number Rhymes* are three of a series of
eight books to remind you of traditional rhymes associated with actions,
published by Ladybird Books, 1976.

The Mouse Book by Helen Piers, Methuen, 1972. Beautifully illustrated
with colour photographs, a first story book which uses question, answer
and repetition to capture the child's interest and involvement; also published as three separate stories (and look for others by this author).

4. BOOKS THAT MIGHT HELP YOUR OTHER
CHILDREN

There are a number of books now which either explain aspects of handicap
for young children, or tell a story which involves a handicapped child and
(usually) his brothers and sisters. Here are a few. The age-ranges given are
only rough guides.

Explaining books, illustrated by colour photographs
Claire and Emma by Diana Peter (on deafness), 1976; *Sally Can't See* by
Palle Peterson (on blindness), English text 1976 (original Danish text
1975); *Janet at School* by Paul White (on spina bifida), 1978; *Don't forget
Tom* by Hanne Larsen (on brain damage), English text 1975 (original
Danish text 1974). All published by Adam and Charles Black. Age 4–10.
Rachel by Elizabeth Fanshawe (on a wheelchair child), 1975; *The Boy Who
Couldn't Hear* by Freddy Bloom, 1977; Bodley Head. Age 4–10.
Lisa and her Soundless World by Edna Levine, Human Sciences Press, 1974.
Very illuminating on deafness. Age 6–11.
I can't talk like you by Althea, Dinosaur Publications, 1982. Written from a
language-impaired child's viewpoint.

Story books
One Little Girl by Joan Fassler, Human Sciences, 1969. A somewhat slow
child: puts her point of view. Age 6–10.
My Brother Barry by Bill Gillham, Andre Deutsch, 1981. Includes a slow-
learning child. Age about 7–11.
The Raft by Alison Morgan, Abelard Schuman, 1974. Includes a physically
disabled child of the 'thalidomide' type. Age about 7–12.
Mark's Wheelchair Adventures by Camilla Jessell, Methuen, 1975. Physically disabled children, much information wrapped in photographically
illustrated story. Age about 8–13.
Let the Balloon Go by Ivan Southall, Methuen, 1968. Child with mild cerebral palsy. Age about 9–14.
Mister O'Brien by Prudence Andrew, Heinemann, 1972. Child with one leg
in calipers. Age about 10–14.
Welcome Home, Jellybean by Marlene Shyer, Granada, 1981. About the
return home of an institutionalised mentally handicapped 13-year-old girl,
seen through the eyes of her younger brother. American setting; pulls no
punches. Age about 10–15.
The October Child by Eleanor Spence, Oxford University Press, 1976.
About an autistic child and his effect on the lives of his elder brothers and
sister. Doesn't side-step the problems. Age about 11–16.
Please don't say Hello by Phyllis Gold, Human Sciences Press, 1976. Focuses
more on the autistic child than the problems he creates. Age about 11–16.
'I own the Racecourse!' by Patricia Wrightson, Hutchinson, 1972 (first published 1968). Hero is a slow-learning boy. Age about 11–16.

Appendix 3 Where to get help: some useful addresses

The addresses given here are of national bodies; there may be very good local help available in your area, which we cannot pinpoint for you here. Local people and organisations who might give you information on resources in your area are: your health visitor; Citizen's Advice Bureau; School Psychological Service or Child Guidance Service (ask at your Local Authority main office); Social Services Department. There is likely to be a branch of MENCAP and a toy library near you: ask at the head offices (addresses below) if you can't find out where.

If you still need more information, try the Voluntary Council for Handicapped Children, which offers an information service and is part of the National Children's Bureau at 8 Wakley Street, London, EC1V 7QE, telephone 01–278–9441. They publish a guide to finding help, *Help Starts Here*, as well as a number of very useful fact sheets – including one on societies for the less common handicaps. Another useful information service is offered by the British Institute of Mental Handicap (Wolverhampton Road, Kidderminster, DY10 3PP), which also runs courses on handicap.

Write to the Family Fund (The Secretary, Box 50, York) for details of special grants for things that might make it easier for you to cope with your child; and to the Toy Libraries Association (Seabrook House, Wyllyotts Manor, Darkes Lane, Potters Bar, Hertfordshire) for a list of toy libraries and for their booklets on helping children to play.

Four major voluntary societies are:

MENCAP (National Society for Mentally Handicapped Children), Pembridge Hall, 12 Pembridge Square, London, W2.

The Spastics Society, 12 Park Crescent, London, W1.

National Society for Autistic Children, 1A Golders Green Road, London, NW11.

Downs Children's Association, Quinbourne Community Centre, Ridgacre Road, Birmingham B32 2TW.

128

Appendix 4 Using this book in a workshop

In designing this book, we have particularly kept in mind that it might be helpful as a handbook for groups of people – parents and professionals – meeting together as a workshop. However, there are no particular rules as to how it should be used. For example, it may be decided that Chapters 1–6 can be presented in a comparatively formal manner, while Chapters 7–10 could be read as 'homework' and brought to the workshop group for discussion. Many of the 'So what now?' sections (especially for Chapters 1, 2, 3, 4 and 6) contain items which can be used effectively in a group without having been looked at before. Others perhaps require more study or thought and can best be read at home following the presentation of the first part of the chapter, and brought back to the group for a feedback session before the next chapter is tackled.

Some of the issues which anyone wishing to set up a workshop might usefully consider are:

TIME FOR EACH SESSION

Much will depend on how much of the formal content of the chapters will be studied in the group. A rough guide would be two hours for each chapter studied, or one hour for discussion of chapters read at home. However, Chapters 1 and 2 can in practice be combined if time is short.

MAKE-UP AND LEADERSHIP OF THE GROUP

Some groups will be much more accustomed to reading or studying than others. These groups may not need either a formal presentation of material or a formal leader. For some relatively self-propelling groups, a rota of 'leaders' could be organised, each being responsible for the study of particular chapters. On the other hand, other groups may need a more structured approach with a regular leader who 'presents' each session in such a way that major points are covered before being read by group members and followed up in the 'So what now?'.

It is likely, perhaps, that the group will be led by a professional. We have found over time that it is easy for people who are dealing in abstract concepts in their daily work to under-estimate the difficulties experienced with these by people who mainly work with practical problems, however intelligent they may be. We have therefore tried to keep the language as simple as possible, given the complexity of some of the concepts, and would point out that it is still much more difficult than the normal reading matter of most of the population. Nonetheless, parents' motivation is usually so high that these difficulties can (in our experience) be overcome even by people who have not attended any class since they left school at 15 or 16.

PRESENTATION OF THE CHAPTERS

Group members need to be aware of the content of the first part in each chapter before any detailed discussion of the exercises in the 'So what now?' sections. The content can be presented in a number of ways, from a formal lecture by the group leader, to each member reading the chapter in advance. This will obviously depend on the needs of the group. Our personal preference is for an informal presentation of each first half by a permanent or rotating leader, followed by discussion to clarify, followed by a 'guided tour' of the practical section, completed by review at home and a feedback period at the beginning of the next session. Where members are at first reluctant to talk in the larger group, the leader could usefully look for opportunities for dividing the group into threes to discuss issues (e.g. What makes us learn? What kinds of learning go into play? What kinds of emotions do parents of handicapped children feel?) and feed them back to the group, to be taken up and structured by the leader; one would expect this to become less necessary as the group gains in cohesiveness.

It is not essential that the order of the chapters is retained precisely as here. However, Chapters 1–6 form a core course, and do need to be presented as a sequence. Chapters 7 and 8 are also an integrated pair. With these provisos, there is no particular reason why the order should not be changed; and in fact Chapter 10 has been very successfully presented first in a workshop course, instead of last.

THE BALANCE BETWEEN ISSUES
AND INDIVIDUAL CASES

The aim of this book is to introduce a way of thinking which can be applied in practice by anyone living or working with a mentally handicapped child. It is therefore very useful – perhaps essential – that every group member has in mind a particular child when studying the chapters. It can be particularly fruitful if individual children can be videotaped in their homes and the results shared with the group as a focus for discussion. The group leader has to maintain a careful balance between the group members' desire to discuss the details of individual cases and the need to retain the structure and sequence of the course as a whole. It may be a good idea to set aside a certain amount of time in each session for the discussion of individual cases – and stick firmly to it! – or to select one or two individual cases which the group agrees will be the focus for the group as a whole when discussing how particular ideas can be applied.

Index

This index is provided so that particular topics can be found wherever they occur; for major topics ('development', 'reward', 'play' for instance), see the contents list.

133

Index